Looking homeward . . .

REPORTS FROM THE HOMEFRONT LINE

R. F. Smith Jr.

FIRST BAPTIST CHURCH

PUBLISHED BY
BRENTWOOD CHRISTIAN PRESS
COLUMBUS, GEORGIA 31907

Looking homeward . . .

REPORTS FROM THE HOMEFRONT LINE

R. F. Smith Jr.

ISBN 1-55630-039-5

Reports
From the Homefront Lines

Acknowledgments

Writers may write alone, but no writer publishes alone. I am indebted to many people who have shared themselves in making this book possible.

Among them: The Rev. John A. Holt, confidant and manuscript reader whose valued suggestions are reflected throughout the book; to Becky Godbey, my secretary, whose patience enabled respect for deadlines and whose diligence made possible the final manuscript; to Barbara Thompson, who typed and retyped the original manuscript with quiet commitment; to Nancy Morrison, whose patience in reading galley proofs relieved pressure as well as provided corrections, and a host of others whose constant persistence for the book finally proved inspirational to me.

I especially want to thank Charles Deal, editor of the *Hickory News*, who not only encouraged me to write a weekly column for his paper, but had the courage to publish it faithfully. He was my mentor and "starter" of weekly reports from the "Homefront Lines."

Some of the material contained in the book appeared in *The Columns*, Fifth Avenue Baptist Church's Weekly newsletter, and some material has appeared in newspaper columns I have written over the years in various newspapers.

-R.F. Smith, Jr.

Foreword

The following pages are "reports from the homefront lines" where I have lived as a child, husband, father, and minister. Written over a period of several years, they reflect the high and low moments of life — and all in between. They are views and perspectives of one person's pilgrimage through the human condition; a journey that is frequently punctuated with question marks of sorrow and burden.

The "reports," written weekly, give sight (if not always insight) into various phases through which families pass. Sometimes the insight blurs, even as the phases blur; but, that is daily family life that is ever so daily.

There are no giant discoveries, but rather little shafts of light that break through onto families in the normal run of duty. The "wheel has not been re-invented," but only greased in moments of squeakingness, hoping that somehow it will make it to the next watering hole.

Grouping the reports has been difficult because family does not happen in formal outline or neat packages. It comes in spurts, alternately hurting and helping; crying and laughing; growing and shrinking, and running and falling.

Continuity of the "reports" is found in the reality of experiences, not in the formal presentation of them. They hang together only in the sense history hangs together; not by refined logic, but by raw reality discovered often in unrelated events and later chronicled by perspective that comes only from reflection.

Yet, unlike logged history that enjoys the luxury of objective distance, they are more akin to the evening news, footnoted sometimes by a quick commentary expressed without benefit of ivory tower detachment; more reaction than response.

And, like the evening news, they are best taken in small time-slots, allowing time for reflection so each person can create commentary.

These "reports from the homefront lines" come through a "reporter" who experienced childhood and teenage years in a home where God was honored and love expressed. Then, in 1955, Faye and I were married and birthed three children — normal and healthy — who dealt with the challenges of life common to all children.

But, unlike most people, yet like far too many, we lost our only son, Forest, who died from a water skiing accident at age seventeen. We have never been the same.

These "reports" are shared with the hope and prayer that your HOMEFRONT LINES will experience the realities of love and living that can come by LOOKING HOMEWARD.

Dedication

To

Faye

For three decades of sharing

The HOMEFRONT LINE

In closeness, openness, and love;

And

To

Becky, Forest, and Rachel

For giving the HOME FRONT LINE

new lines of insight, challenge, and love

plus cause for HOMEFRONT pride;

And

To

Ophelia and Forest,

Mom and Dad,

For love and courage

To rear a son,

especially during the Great Depression.

About the Writer . . .

Dr. R.F. Smith, Jr., Senior Minister of the Fifth Avenue Baptist Church, Huntington, West Virginia, is a native of North Carolina where he was ordained in 1953 and served churches for over twenty-five years, including the pulpits of First Baptist Churches in Durham, Hickory, North Wilkesboro, and Pittsboro. He served as a communications consultant in the marketplace for two years prior to assuming his present pastorate in 1979.

He was graduated from Wake Forest University and Southeastern Baptist Seminary and has served as trustee of both institutions. He holds both earned and honorary doctorates.

During his ministry he has served both the Southern Baptist Convention and the American Baptist Churches, USA in various leadership roles.

Dr. Smith's writings appear in newspapers regularly. He writes for the Kiester-Williams Newspaper Services, a syndicate that places his writings in 1000 newspapers weekly with a readership of over 60 million.

He served as Preacher-of-the-Week at the famous Chautauqua Institute in New York in 1983. As schedule permits, he continues to speak in the marketplace, at business and professional conventions, seminars, workshops, as well as college campuses.

The Fifth Avenue Pulpit enables him to preach weekly to a congregation of university and townspeople who reflect a healthy cross-section of society.

He is married to the former Miss Faye Tyndall. They reared three children: Becky, born 1958; Forest, born 1960, deceased 1978, and Rachel, born 1962.

Starting
the
Line

Love and Marriage

Starting the Line
(Love and Marriage)
Love Half-Price

I was in a hurry as I dashed for the front door of a drug store, but was stopped dead in my tracks by the big, hand-painted sign that boldly announced: "Love ½ Price."

All sorts of reactions surfaced in the split seconds I pondered that sign. Then I discovered what the sign meant. A cosmetic, brand-named LOVE, was on sale for half-price. But the sign has kept gnawing at me. Love ½ Price!

The first thing that hits me is that love cannot be bought at any price. It is a gift. It is something another person bestows upon me, entrusts with me, and risks on me. There's no way I can purchase it on the common market in consumer packages at cut-rate prices. It never goes on sale.

Love is not a cosmetic that covers my bumps and warts, or removes aging wrinkles from my face. It is an indefinable quality that accepts me, warts and all; and its warmness, while not removing the wrinkles, nevertheless causes the wrinkles to crease into smiles that rise from a heart that pulsates in a strange rhythm that only love can stimulate.

Love is not a lipstick but a walking cane that props me up on my leaning side.

Love is not a rouge that gives color to my face; it is a face that brings color to my life when smiling at me.

Love is not eye shadow; it is eyes that see deep into my soul, removing shadows that bring fear.

Love is not make-up that covers me; it is a covering, a security, that makes me into what I can be when loved and challenged by love.

Yet, there's a real sense in which love costs. It demands investment of time, talent, treasure. It costs emotional energy, mental contribution, spiritual power, and physical strength.

Love does not come cheap. While it cannot be bought, it must, however, be purchased at the enormous price of total commitment. It requires hours of conversation with the loved one, an openness that permits another to look inside, even walk inside; and it requires a risk that dares respond with total resources.

Love costs! But it can never be purchased on the open market and popular prices, let alone at half-price!

Love is a gift that defies all principles of economy, because the more I give away the more I have. A business would fail operating on such a principle; but love becomes bankrupt if it does not!

And on Fourth-and-Ten

He was a football player, and was getting married. Like many young people today, the couple had written part of the wedding ceremony.

Standing in the university chapel where he had received his degree only a week before, he promised in sacred vows many things to his bride, all in fresh, new language.

Then came the clincher: "Betty," he intoned. "I promise you that even with my back against the goal line, I will not punt on fourth-and-ten!"

What a promise! And commitment! That's about as much commitment as you can put into one sentence. No quarterback in his right mind, at least early in the game, would do such a thing, make such a promise.

When you get into that position in a football game, you've got only one thought — get out of there the best way you can. Kick that ball as far as possible.

What was the young football player promising with such a statement? He was saying, I think, that when everything nailed down in the marriage seems to be coming loose, he will not give up. He will try to find one plank, one sturdy board, he can cling to.

He was saying that when pressures and stresses seem to press in from all sides, he will not sacrifice his marriage on the altar of expediency.

I think he meant that winning the game is not nearly so important as being counted on to keep hitting the line regardless of the odds.

Could be he intends to go against the grain of popular procedures if his marriage gets into trouble.

I think his statement shows insight into marriage. He at least perceives that there will be fourth-and-ten situations, that everything will not be first-and-ten.

Perhaps he learned early in his football experience that it's easy to score a touchdown, but difficult to be splattered by the opposing team, then get up, brush yourself off, and go at it again.

And maybe, just maybe, he knew that marriage is much like a footbal game: rules, guidelines, penalties, game plans, failures, restrictions, discipline, all designed to make the game real and exciting, not to prohibit freedom or curtail joy.

That's not a bad commitment to put into the marriage ceremony, and marriage. "I will not punt, even if my back is against the goal line, on fourth-and-ten."

Metal and Marriage

"Don't look while I'm welding this," the man with the welding torch told me just before pulling the protective shield over his eyes. "It'll ruin your eyes," he advised, and I closed my eyes while he welded my wagon back together. "Will it break again?" I asked, as he cooled the hot spot and pushed my vehicle back to me.

"No, not there. That's the strongest part of your wagon. You may break it somewhere else, but never where it's been welded."

I was about ten-years-old when I first heard that bit of practical philosophy, and I've heard it many times since.

It's a philosophy that holds true in many experiences in life, especially in relationships.

This is a basic principle in the marriage relationship and experience. When a "break" comes in the marriage, and the couple seeks qualified help in working through the causes for the break, the "welded marriage" is often stronger, not because of the break but because they worked through problems that may have plagued the marriage for years.

14

But there's a difference in welding a piece of metal and a marriage. You dare not look at the brightness of a welder's torch, but in a marriage-break you had better look at whatever light is turned on the breakage. In short, facing up to the problems that caused the break is the only way healing can happen.

"She won't even look at the situation," or "He refuses to admit we have a problem," are statements that render marriage-breaks hopeless, making any attempt at healing and welding impossible.

Another hopeless situation exists when one or the other marriage partners says, "I want help with our marriage but he/she refuses. I'm not going to seek help alone!"

My suggestion: Go! If your partner refuses, that's his/her problem. But you have a responsibility to and for yourself. Counseling will help you, and in time your mate may consent to go.

When a break occurs in marriage someone had better take the initiative and seek help. Marriage-breaks, like toothaches, may go away for a time. But ultimately the tooth (marriage-break) must be dealt with.

And the comforting, reassuring fact is: The welded part becomes the strongest part of the metal, and the marriage.

No Rivets

One of my favorite writers produced a blooper recently. (Guess that makes him as human as the rest of us?) He said, "A baby is a little rivet in the bonds of matrimony."

He didn't think long enough on that one. A baby coming into a breaking or broken marriage is not a rivet that strengthens the bond; not if the bond needs welding.

The child can become a wedge at worst and an idol at best. No child can solve marriage problems, but often becomes a pawn in a doomed chess game.

Yet many couples, nursing a shaky marriage, honestly believe that a baby can solve all sorts of adult problems. Children are miracles, but cannot perform miracles.

Having a baby in the midst of marital unrest will create excitement and provide diversion, just as any new novelty will relieve boredom and forestall positive action.

But relief and delay are not solutions; fact is, they often retard solutions, creating a false sense of security that can blow up on any given day.

The answer to marriage problems is not found in birthing a baby, but in birthing roads to professional persons who can help husband and wife unlock some of the problems that imprison them.

No child has such power, and to expect a child to solve adult problems is as stupid as it is impossible. Children have a tendency to blame themselves when their fathers and mothers split up. They often make childish but sincere efforts to mend the marriage. And when they fail, they blame themselves.

Now, if parents expect the child to heal the wounds — and the child himself expects this of himself — you don't have to be a psychologist to figure out the overwhelming pressure and guilt the child feels.

Your child can never solve your marriage problems. He is not a rivet in the bonds of matrimony. He is a child, dependent on the two people who brought him (unrequested) into the world for security, guidance, and love.

The
Line
Starts
Children

The Line Starts
(Children)
Not Little Adults

One evening we were entertaining friends. Our Children (pre-school then) were safely tucked in bed, or so we thought. The oldest appeared in the doorway, crooked her finger and motion-ed for me.

"Come on in, honey," I invited. In a loud whisper she told me her sister was sick.

One of the guests, a young internist physician, was urged by his wife to go with me to see what could be done. He looked at the child, made some doctor-motions, and said, shaking his head, "I don't know. I think you ought to call the child's doc-tor. I'm not that familiar with treating children."

I must have looked at him rather confused-like. He elaborated. "Children are not just little adults, you know." This statement has been ringing in my ears ever since. I must admit that over the years I have sometimes forgotten the truth of the young doctor's statement, especially during times of my own frustration over what our children have done or have not done.

Children are not "just little adults" physically, and they are not just little adults mentally, emotionally, or spiritually. Sometimes we forget those facts, too!

I firmly believe that we should have high expectations of our children. We should call-out the best that's in them, and should help them realize their potentialities.

But UNREAL-DEMANDS ARE A DIFFERENT ballgame than high expectations. And it's at the point of unreal-demands that children can suffer emotional and spiritual damage.

High expectations stimulate self-motivation; unreal-demands stiffle creativity.

High expectations call forth the best; unreal-demands push back the best.

High expectations prompt goal-motivation; unreal-demands generate fear-motivation.

High expectations dramatize reachable dreams; unreal-demands drum out dreams and usher in nightmares.

High expectations give hearts warmth; unreal-demands give stomach ulcers.

High expectations, well, they lift to heaven; unreal-demands are hellish, making a hell of every heaven.

A Sense of Wonder

What's it like to be a child? It's been a long time since I was one, but I have some friends who are. And they shed light on that subject from time to time.

It's to have a SENSE OF WONDER. You can see it in their eyes, hear it in their questions, and know it from the way they get excited.

I have a new young friend named Matt. He's five-years-old, and the sense of wonder in him is dynamic. Matt has a way of "putting things" with words.

The other day when beautiful white clouds formed all sorts of imaginable animals against a blue backdrop, Matt said to his mother, "Could we drive down the road and see if any clouds have run out of breath and fallen?"

"Have you ever seen a fallen cloud, Matt?" mother asked.

"One time I saw a cloud caught in top of a tree, and another time I saw one floating on the river," Matt allowed, and kept looking at the sky, wondering about the clouds.

During Matt's toilet training days he sneezed and liberally sprayed his pajama bottom. He went to his mother and explained. "Mommie, I didn't wet my 'jamas, I just bless-you'd all over them."

To be a child is to be a poet, using the sense of wonder as lyrics for the building of thoughts, thoughts that often lie too deep for words.

A child is a person who lives in a forest of legs and knees. That's all he sees of adults, unless he risks breaking his neck by bending way-back to look up at the tall timbers that surround him.

Suggestion: when talking with a child, stoop down to his eye level. You'll be amazed how that opens up all sorts of communication possibilities.

A child is impressed by little things, like a funny-shaped stick that resembles something his mind conjures up, firing his imagination.

And big, important (to adults, that is) things leave him untouched, unmoved. A house is a house, a car is a car, a chair is a chair, and time is something that has no beginning and certainly no ending!

His sense of wonder makes an ocean of a bathtub, complete with a marineland of creatures; a pile of leaves becomes a space walk; a mudhole is transformed into clay fit for a sculptor; chairs with blankets draped over them become a castle to be defended at any cost.

And life is pretty wonderful.

There's Another Way . . .

He was about nine. That growing, learning, investigating, getting-into-trouble age.

"Dad," he said, as I walked by his room. "Would you come in a minute. Got something to tell you."

I settled on the foot of his bed and picked up a loose football trying to escape down the too-small crack between his bed and wall. He was stretched out on the bed with hands interlaced behind his head. We were comfortable.

"Dad, this guy at school is giving me a hard time again."

"The same one?" I asked, remembering other conversations about him.

"Yeah, the same guy. He shoves me every time he gets a chance. I'm getting tired of it."

We talked on a bit. I said little that was definite, trying to stimulate his thinking and not giving any answers. (Maybe I didn't have any.)

"Today he really made me mad. Called me names and hit me on the back — real hard — just as I walked through the door into a classroom."

I didn't say anything. Actually, I was becoming a bit angry

because he had not stood up for himself.

He stopped talking. Dead silence.

Then he said, "What are YOU going to do about it?"

"What am I going to do about it? It's your problem."

"You mean," he said and raised up on the bed, "you're not going to help me out? You're not going to do anything?"

Maybe I was tired. It had been a long day. I don't know. But I was getting upset with him. Why doesn't he assert himself? I thought. He needs to be more aggressive, I argued to myself.

"No, it's your problem. I'll help you look at the things you can do. But the final decision is yours. You'll have to decide what you're going to do; how you're going to handle it."

"What can I do?" he wanted to know.

My anger surfaced.

"You've got two choices. You can stand up and fight him or lie down and let him walk over you!"

Then his anger surfaced. "That's the way YOU would do it," and his eyes flashed. "You'd fight, wouldn't you?"

I didn't answer.

"Go on, tell me. You'd fight, wouldn"t you?"

I calmed down a bit. "I told you I'd help you look at the ways you could handle this. That's all I'm going to do. I'll say it again. You've got two choices: fight or flight."

"No," he said, and anger really came out. "There's a third way. I can make him my friend. You would never have thought of that," his anger flashed and he dashed out the door.

I sat there a long time. Fight . . . flight . . . friend. Makes sense.

"And a little child shall lead them . . ."

That's what he did; they became friends.

How Home Happens

Home happens when honesty is in residence. Family is a group of people who have enough integrity of mind and spirit to say at times, "There are some things I cannot fix for you."

When "new math" appeared on the academic scene, I simply told our children that I could not help them. If they could use "old math" I would be of some help. But I admitted that I didn't know the new stuff and had no inclination to learn it.

21

There have been many other times in our children's lives when honesty demanded that I say, "I don't know. I can't fix it for you. I will cry with you, listen to you, but there are some things that dad, with all his love for you, cannot fix."

Honesty also demands, as someone suggested, that we learn when to pat each other and with what to pat each other, and on which end!

Confrontation "in love" is often called for in family. The use of such words as No, Wait, Maybe, and Perhaps may be more important than positive Yeses and permissiveness that produces over-indulged off-springs who have more foliage than root.

Home happens when each person feels sheltered from life's storms.

For a small child a storm may be the loss of a pet. When our German Shepherd died we drove to my family homeplace, there to lay to rest the dog the children had grown up with.

As I placed the last shovel of dirt tenderly over the mound, they said, "Dad, will you say something over him?" and tears streamed down their faces.

Genuinely and tenderly as I could, I prayed, thanking God for the gift of animals who love us and teach us, even in their so-called dumb state, what love is.

Children are too young to meet loss alone. (For that matter, is anyone ever old enough to face loss alone?)

Teenagers appear seldom to need much family, except to rebel and complain about. But don't let them fool you. They need familiar landscape — faces, furniture, fixtures — when storms come and decisions must be faced.

Adults need family, too: a place and a group in which they draw strength from each other. Home happens when we feel loved, accepted, and secure amid life's storms.

Not a Thing

It's not the most beautiful creation in the world, but for the past twenty-plus years it has occupied a prominent place in my study room at home.

The materials are as simple as the creative product: an empty toilet paper cylinder wrapped with a scrap piece of shelving contact paper and mounted on a plaster cast about two inches in diameter. Cost? About ten percent of nothing!

But I hold it in high, sentimental esteem.

Why? Because our first-born made it in kindergarten and proudly brought it to me with a smile I can still see. "It's for you, daddy," she announced with genuine joy. "It's a pencil holder," she explained and started stuffing my loose pencils into it. "And you can put your rubber bands around it," she instructed as she set it beside my telephone, in easy reach.

What she made was more than a thing, more than a pencil holder. It was an extension of herself. She was joyfully expressing herself in what she was producing. The psychologist would say she was having her humaness enhanced.

And it was tremendously important that I took seriously, and with appreciation, her production. In the process of creating that pencil holder she was investing herself, her sense of worth and creativity. It was not merely a product; it was a part of herself she was giving to me.

It stands there now (still by the telephone, still filled with pencils and wrapped with rubber bands) as a silent symbol that on a special day when she was five-years-old, she gave me a special part of herself.

Almost every week I receive "works of art" from children. They present me with crayon drawings often lettered with wiggly lines and backward-made letters. Such creations will never hang in art galleries, but in the gallery of my own appreciation they hang with dignity because I know the children are saying to me: "This is who I am; this is how I feel; this is part of me. And I love you."

We are all children who have grown bigger. Our work is but the expansion of ourselves through creativity. And when we fail to experience childlike excitement in what we do, something sacred is lost.

Everybody's Doing It!

"He's a good kid." That's what the father told me. "'Bout sixteen — the driver-license age. Trust him totally. Never made the drug scene. Decent grades. Works hard at studies."

"That's great," I told him. "Lots of parents would give anything to be in your shoes."

He talked on about his son. Goes to church, reads his Bible, a good thinker.

"One day we had a long talk," the father related. "Told him I was proud of him. Proud he did not feel he had to 'go with the crowd.'"

"Not going with the crowd takes a lot of backbone," I suggested.

"It does," he agreed. "I told him he didn't have to do everything everybody else does. The mark of maturity, I told him, is being able to go against popular trends."

Our conversation lasted a long time. We traded ideas about rearing children. Both agreed parenting is the biggest challenge and thrill any human being can experience.

As we started to leave the sandwich bar where we had drained several cups of coffee, he wrinkled his face in something of a frown. Sat back as if not through. I sat back too.

"The other day he hit me broadside. Know what he said?" I didn't and shook my head that way.

"We were talking about something, can't remember what. I was a little ticked-off at him. Then I really blew it. Man, did I ever blow it."

I was on the edge of my seat, just dying to know what he had blown.

"I was angry. A little bit, maybe. Here's what I said: 'Why don't you do so-and-so. Every other boy your age does. Just about everyone!!'"

"He looked hurt. I've never seen his eyes like that before. His look stunned me. But his statement woke me up."

"'Dad,' he said slowly as if he didn't believe he had heard me say what I said. 'You've always told me not to go with the crowd. You've never let me use the excuse that everybody is doing it. You've always told me I am a person. Told me to act as an individual. That I am an original and not mess my life up being a carbon copy of anybody.

"'Now you are going against everything you've taught me. Do you want me to do everything everybody else is doing?'"

"He was sincere, not just arguing. I put my arm around him. Asked forgiveness for my slip of reason and reality. He smiled. Not a smile of victory, but of relief."

Conversation was over; coffee gone. I walked alone down the

street. The thought wouldn't leave. It bounced around for awhile. Still with me. Amazing how we congratulate our kids for not being like everyone else when they please us. Amusing how we want them to be like everyone else when they displease us.

Courage to be Impractical (at times)

"He is so practical that life with him gets boring at times." In counseling I've heard that statement over and over, from husbands and wives (and children).

Why not be impractical, at least at times? Well, it takes courage. And some risking. People will shake their heads in wonderment. But it's worth it.

In January, 1978, about mid-morning, our seventeen-year-old son and I were driving back from an errand. Several inches of snow lay on the ground, but the roads were clear.

"Dad," he said. "I bet there's a lot of snow up in the mountains. Our snow tires would get us there. Just forty miles away. How 'bout it?"

I looked at the excitement in his eyes. "Why not?" I said, turning the car into the driveway.

"Mom could fix us a picnic," he said loudly, jumping out of the car and hurrying to con his mother out of a big lunch.

As we drove into the mountains the snow got deeper, and his excitement became louder with every new inch of snow we encountered. We both enjoyed every minute of it. Finding a deserted parking lot at a summer amusement park, we stopped for lunch under a covered picnic area beside a half-frozen mountain stream struggling to flow.

Coldness soon drove us back into the car to finish our lunch. Then he took the driver's seat, and in the big lot, spun the car around many times as we pretended to be on a slick race track. After driving on the worst snow-covered roads we could find, we headed home. He took a nap in the backseat as the low lands turned snow into water.

"Dad, that was fun. Thanks," he said as we unloaded our gear in the basement.

Eight months later he was dead, victim of a water skiing accident. As I write this, snow is on the ground. Yes, the snow kicks up all sorts of sad feelings, but the feelings would be sadder had I not been impractical that snowy, January morning and took a day to be with my son and share his excitement over playing in snow.

Snow flakes will always remind me of him and the day we were so impractical.

Being impractical, at times, with our kids could give them a basis for understanding us! If we want our kids to be adults sometime, then sometimes we must be kids with them.

And TODAY is the only "for-sure day" we have.

Ain't Nothing Last Forever

I was down in Georgia; had just finished speaking. A mother, in her forties, wanted to talk with me. Something I had said triggered a memory.

"What you said about living in a wilderness reminded me of something my elderly aunt told me years ago.

"I had been called home to help nurse my dying father, and had taken our four small children with me. It had been a long day. Dad so sick ... children restless, tired. I was at wits' end.

"My aunt, rocking on the porch, took it all in. She relieved her overflowing snuff in the little can beside her chair and said, 'Honey, ain't nothing lasts forever!'"

I find that statement both comforting and saddening. The comfort comes when days drag by on leaden feet of frustration and discouragement and other negative goodies. It's good to know, "Ain't nothing lasts forever." Good to know we don"t live our lives forever in valleys and wildernesses; there are some mountain peaks if we can just hang on and hang tough.

Yet there's a sadness in its truth: the beauty of childhood flourishing and then fading all too soon. Seeing their sense of wonder when a wave of never-before-seen ocean breaks on their little bodies and they leap into tanned arms for security.

Their prideful laughter when they solo ten feet on the bike minus its training wheels.

And their feeling of self-worth when they knock their first ball over dad's head and he scrambles amidst their childish giggles to rescue it before his prize rose bush becomes victim.

"Ain't nothing lasts forever." The statement hurts.

The highly-charged atmosphere of excitement on Christmas

Eve and even higher-charged little minds that fretfully stir through a sleep-won't-come-night.

Standing at the head of the steps — chomping at the bits of a five o'clock gate-opening — knocking on your door every two minutes ("When are you coming?"), and you wonder if even the angels are up at such an ungodly hour.

"Ain't nothing lasts forever." And it makes you sad.

The first date . . . and first heartbreak. That first prom . . . and corsage. Driver's license . . . and first bent fender. Bicycles gathering dust. Dolls stored. Picture-story books filed (rescued from garage sale at last sentimental moment). Picnics . . . touch-football . . . romps in woods . . . kittens born in a closet and watched by young wide-eyes learning "facts-o-life". . . so quiet . . . awed by miracle of life. Worship. Almost.

"Ain't nothing lasts forever." Oh, Stop, Time in your flight . . ."

Long talks . . . subjects getting heavier. Discussion lengthening the nights. Nights broadening the days . . . and communication.

Heartbreaks aired . . . broken romances grieved over . . . tears wetting your shoulders.

Dreams verbalized. Visions verb-ized. Hopes pinned on SAT scores . . . future penned on applications. Eternity knocks. They answer. Rooms emptied. Spare furniture donated to bare little apartments.

"Ain't nothing lasts forever." You turn, walk into the meadow where you can think — and remember. And you remember. You remember: "Ain't nothing lasts forever." You're glad. And sad.

Holding
the
Line

Parenting

Holding the Line
(Parenting)
Having and Giving

Television commercials intrigue me. Some are pure genius; others pure stupidity. All of them contain philosophy, some of it bad. Others contain some theology, often bad.

There is one produced by a money-lending agency which sings a little jingle that jumps out at me. By borrowing money from them, or investing money with them, you can enjoy: "Giving your children what you never had," or so they sing.

Can you really do that? Can you actually give your children what you never had?

In some areas, yes. We can give them "things" we never had; material possession such as cars, clothes, trips. And we can give them TIME. That is, we can be with them more than our parents were with us. And that's an important gift.

But can we give them a value system we've never had? Can we pass on to them spiritual and moral values we've never had?

Can we give them a faith we've never had?

Can we give our children integrity we've never possessed? Or morality? Or a sense of wonder? Or a sense of the eternal? No. I doubt we can give any person any of these great moral values we've never experienced.

We can give only those things we possess as ours, or only those things that are being born within us and we are in process of experiencing.

But all is not lost. We can develop these values along with our children. We can grow. Just because we've never had these great values in our lives does not mean we are up some theological or philosophical moral creek without a paddle. A worthy value system is available to parents if discipline, desire, and commitment accompany efforts to develop these attributes.

It boils down to a willingness to pay the price of growing, and allowing these moral values to birth within us. Then we can pass them along and share them with our children who look to us for leadership by EXAMPLE.

The price of a costly home extracts from us the price of genuine commitment; to achieve in our lives a degree of maturity that enables us to give our children what we possess because we have experienced and practiced a vital system of values.

We cannot really "give our children what we've never had." But we can get "what we've never had." Then we can pass it along.

"No! I Love You!"

She was about three when it happened. And our youngest. Being the youngest she perhaps needed extra assurance. But the youngest to the oldest in every family asks the same question many, many times. Maybe not in the same way, but they ask it.

The conversation went something like this:

"Daddy, (or 'Diddy' as she pronounced it). Can I go out and play?" (It was raining cats and dogs.)

"Surely," I said, putting her on a bit. "You can go out."

"But it's raining out there," she protested.

"I know."

"But I'll get wet," she argued.

"Yep, you probably will," I calmly replied.

"I might get sick, too!" she frustratedly explained.

"That could happen," I suggested.

And then with a real trace of hurt in her voice she said, "You don't love me!"

Children do not usually explain their often outlandish requests and actions in such transparent openness. They are a bit more subtle and veiled. But the motivation is the same. They want to know they are loved.

Rebellion, defiance, and antagonism are often nothing more or less than an attempt to learn if they are loved.

Often they "test" parents to see how far the parents will allow them to go before they hear a good, solid "No!" And that

"No!" says: "I love you." Oh, they will fume, fuss and want to fight about it; but deep down inside they have heard what they wanted to hear.

Restrictions, regulations — these become the backboard against which a child can rebound without fear of going out of the "court of play."

Over-permissiveness is not necessarily an expression of love; it may be the opposite. On the other hand, being overly strict or coercive does not "shout out" love either. It may be spawned by the parents' inner fears, frustrations or insecurities.

Somewhere between the two extremes, as Aristotle reminded us, lies the virtue of loving and the even greater virtue of letting our children know they are loved.

Behind You

It was one of those fun-times for their family, the mother told me. Nestled away in a remote summer cottage, far from jangling, jarring phone bells, the family was frolicking in fun-things.

Life was moving slower, more in pace with the soul than in step with the fast-track they live on most of the time. Reflection replaced rigid schedules and enabled minds to wander in uncharted territory, granting freedom for newly freed spirits.

The father had taken their youngest, a cute and refreshing nine-year-old, and several of her peers on a walking trip down back of the cottage to investigate the wild things that grow and live there.

Darkness came and only added to the adventure, stirring up fantasy monsters that any nine-year-old mind can entertain without even half-trying.

"Daddy," she called as they turned to make their way back up the winding trail to home and family. "Can I be the leader?" And with that the father handed her the flashlight.

With light searching out the path, she turned and said to a little friend beside her, "It's fun being the leader when your daddy is behind you."

It's amazing what children can do when they know they have the support (and presence) of parents. When daddy is behind you all sorts of monsters fade from your mind. Why, even dragons can be slain when you know that daddy and mommie are behind you, backing you up and giving you courage by the knowledge that "they are there."

And when you get older, into those teenage tightropes, it's still good to know they are behind you. Now you won't come right out and admit that, let alone say it! But, deep down inside, you are glad they are there, handing you whatever flashlight of insight you need for whatever trail you're on.

When the simple trail outback of summer home turns into narrow valleys of twenties and wilderness of thirties on into canyons of mid-life challenges, it's still good to know that in spirit they are still behind you, praying, supporting — and hoping.

Show and Remember

She was about twenty-months-old and fidgeted around the hall while we waited to see the doctor in our small-town clinic. The elevator fascinated her. Each time it opened she would say, "What's that?"

Then it dawned on me! One person would get on and in a few minutes three or four would get off. Blacks would get on and whites would get off.

And in the mind of a child can you imagine what was going on? Here's a room that makes three people out of one, and turns blacks into whites!

I took her by the hand and entered the little up-and-down room. We rode and got off on the next floor, walked around, then came back down.

She was satisfied. Her question answered, or at least she never asked it again.

"I treat my son," said a wise father, "as if I'm taking a person on tour of a world he's never seen before." In reality, that's the way it is. Our children have never seen this world before, and what is old-hat to us is excitingly new to them. And sometimes it's scary, too.

"Never tell your child when you can show him," is not only good advice, it's the essence of education, reminding us that a picture is still worth a thousand words.

And if one picture is worth a thousand words, how much

more is "an experience" worth?

I have a deep love and respect for history, implanted in part by a father whose love for the subject moved us each summer from one Civil War battleground to another. What I read in books we traced on foot from battleline to battleline, and I could almost hear the guns firing, commands given, and the throat-rattling yell of Johnny Reb!

Children do not learn in vacuums, dealing with abstract ideas and concepts. They learn in context of experience. Teachable moments usually happen when something touchable is being experienced.

In later years children recall concepts they learned early, and they are often linked to some experience or event. It's common to hear, "I remember one summer at the beach when the storm came, that dad said . . ." Then follows some basic principle of life learned during that exotic or scary time.

Concepts are learned in context, and are recalled because they are tied to some event, some happening.

"Don't tell your child when you can show him."

Rationale for Rules

"My tailor is the wisest man I know," declared George Bernard Shaw. "He's the only person who measures me everytime I go in."

Most of us do not extend such wise courtesy to other people, nor do we receive it. We tend to see people in the same light year in and year out, never suspecting the person has grown and matured.

The temptation to label people by the same size — mentally, emotionally, spiritually — is perhaps greatest in the family, among the people we live with every day.

But people do grow, change and embrace new perspectives. And to perceive them unchanged is gross discourtesy, maybe a crime.

No well-managed business ever operates within rigid structures that fail to move with the times (the market), refusing to update procedures. Business firms ruin, rot and deplete productivity when they attempt to operate with production models never altered. They constantly study and re-negotiate

34

contracts in management, manufacturing, merchandising, and marketing.

Families are also in a business: the business of growing, maturing, and learning to live life, not merely exist through life.

Constant evaluation and re-evaluation are needed in family. Contracts, ground rules, and mutual understandings must be frequently reviewed and re-negotiated.

Such important contracts as money allowances, curfew, study-time, off-limit places of entertainment, bedtime, and other scaffolding of structure should come up for periodic review and be subject to good reasoning and reasons.

Rationale for rules should be high on the agenda of every family intent on providing fertile soil for children to develop self-starting motivations. And legitimate rationale for all rules is imperative if family integrity is maintained.

"That's a rule in this family simply because I said so," is not a good reason or rationale for the rule. As children grow older they deserve to know why certain rules and guidelines exist in the family.

"That's the way we did it in my family and that's the way we'll do it in ours," is not good rationale if the tradition is questioned or contested.

Children change as they grow. Family guidelines should be re-defined and re-negotiated to meet their growth, and parents do well to establish (and defend with integrity) rationale for all rules.

Boys and Bending Nails

People are always passing stories and ideas along to me (and I appreciate it!). Here's one.

The minister asked a group of children in Sunday School, "Why do you love God?" He got a variety of answers.

But the one he liked best was from a boy who said, "I don't know, sir. I guess it just runs in the family."

I like that! Says a lot about family and what happens in family. The home continues to be the basic institution of learning in society.

Some things (many things) just "run in the family."

Children catch the spirit of things, imitate behavior, and become carbon copies of what they experience in the home.

Many times they not only look like us, they act like us. Our value systems become the basis for their values, and this can be both negative and positive.

Children are little tape recorders, storing for all time who we are and what we are. The tapes replay parents' behavior, actions and ideas.

My dad was a craftsman, having built many pieces of furniture that occupy exalted positions in our home. Grandfather clocks have come from his workshop regularly over the years, not copies but his own creative ideas enshrined in solid black walnut.

During my childhood and teenage years I used to help him with projects. Sometimes he would consent to apply his talents for a neighbor whose house needed repair.

I remember one time we were building a new set of steps for a friend. We had driven big nails to hold the thick lumber. Dad told me to crawl under the steps and bend the nails up against the lumber.

"Nobody will ever see those nails, Dad," I argued, not wanting to crawl in the dirt and waste energy on something that did not show.

"Maybe," he said, "But I'll know they are there."

Every time something needs doing in my life that does not "show," and I could "get by" without doing it, the statement by my dad surfaces.

And the statement haunts, plagues, stimulates, and motivates me to add the extra touch, which is always the mark of a craftsman.

I have not always "bent all the nails," but I've never escaped hearing that tape playing when I ignored responsibility.

Some things just run in the family, and in later life those things run the child-now-grown. And that fact is both comforting and disturbing.

Of Dogs and Men

His name was Tarzan and he was born about the same year I came into the world. For seventeen years we were constant companions.

Tarzan was a dog. My grandparents' dog. He had no pedigree and could best be described as a "duke's mixture." But he loved and was loved by the family.

A small fellow, clothed in a brown and white coat, he carried his tail in a question mark circle and wagged it constantly as he went about his dog-life.

Tarzan was known by about everybody in our small town. I'm told that his appearance downtown immediately cleaned up conversations because he was "Preacher Benfield's dog," and the beloved and respected pastor could not be too far behind.

The little dog had many fine points. Often he was left overnight in a grocery store managed by my uncles to catch four-legged, furry varmints that roamed the aisles. Never once did Tarzan help himself to the many cakes and cookies that were his for the taking.

My grandparents had a family ritual they observed every night. Just before going to bed they read the Bible and knelt for prayer. Tarzan was always there. After evening devotions they would lead him to the basement door and he'd go down to his sleeping quarters.

Just for fun I would often try to get the dog to go out before devotions. He wouldn't budge, no matter how intensely I called him.

Sometimes I'd try to pick him up, but the usual non-violent little dog would growl, and I could tell by his tone he meant business.

Then I'd put him down and my grandfather would take his well-worn Bible and read. After we all knelt for prayer, Tarzan would get up, stretch, and go to the basement door. He knew it was bedtime for all.

Our little dog-friend was seventeen when a car struck him, injuring him so badly that it was necessary to "put him to sleep."

We cried when his lifeless little body was placed tenderly in

37

garden ground. And tears came again, many times, when family devotions were over and no Tarzan there to stretch and go to the basement.

If a little dog can be impressed with family rituals, such as Bible reading and prayer, how much more can little children be influenced by rituals that in later years will become more than rituals for them. Daily routines and habits may become the structures of life that will give meaning and reality in a world that could devastate them.

Faults or Faulty?

One of life's greatest gifts is the ability to see people's faults without seeing them as faulty persons. I'm convinced that's not only a gift but a gift that is constantly cultivated.

It is a gift, while not native for some people, that can be purchased on the market of common sense at the nominal cost of sensitive practice.

Maybe it is an art in which we learn to perceive a person's failures without painting them a failure. Or we detect their bad actions and habits without labeling them bad people.

We see demonstrations of such practices on athletic fields and floors all the time. Some coaches coach persons not players, while others coach players rather than persons. And their chosen philosophy dictates their actions.

A young man runs off the field after literally blowing a play. He missed a crucial tackle. A coach, depending upon his basic philosophy, may say one of two things.

"That was a terrible play you just missed. You're better than that. Get back in there and do what you are capable of doing."

Now that's a far cry from the coach who says, "You are terrible — a terrible player. You'll never make it. Never."

In this challenging assignment called life, we all fumble the ball at times. Mistakes are often the mark of honest effort, and failures a real mark of trying. But if we make life's biggest mistake of judging ourselves "a failure" in light of our failures, all is lost. And we trust that friends, teachers, family, and loved ones will not make that big mistake with us or for us.

The Apostle Paul, never one to mince words, had the good

sense and sensitivity to see people's faults with utter clarity and deal with the faults in utter fidelity. He never made the mistake of labeling persons faulty because of their faults.

Faults, failures and mistakes do not make us sub-human. They merely indicate that we are human, and in need of human (sometimes super-human) understanding and help.

Once a Child, Always a Parent

I was standing beside my grandmother at the funeral home when it happened. The wife of one of her seven sons had died. She looked at him, then reached out her arms to embrace him. For a few tender moments mother and son cried in each other's arms.

Then she moved back, looked him tenderly but firmly in the eyes and said, "Son, come home with me. You can't live alone."

That scene may not appear unusual except for the circumstances. You see, she was in her 90's, living in a nursing home, nearly blind and deaf, and only the steady hand of her son kept her from falling when she lifted both arms to embrace him, forgetting her man-made walker that was her constant companion.

We all were moved by the motherly act of compassion, and from some distant philosopher an old phrase surfaced: "You may stop being a child, but you never stop being a parent!"

And the truth of that old adage, while tender, beautiful and heart-warming, creates much trouble in many families. It's difficult to stand back and watch children suffer at the hands of normal growth processes.

The temptation "to do for them" begins early, and finds its first real conflict in the experience of watching them struggle to take that first step. Remember how much you wanted to reach out and help when they tottered, then fell head-first?

It's not easy to maintain a hands-off policy when your own flesh-and-blood hurts, even though you know it is for their own good and growth.

But the essence of healthy family life is found only in the systematic "loss" of children. Because family is an institution that fails when it keeps its product!

Knowing how to strike the proper balance between too much

parenting and too little parenting is a constant struggle for the serious parent. And how to measure this balance is crucial, but delicate.

There are many measuring sticks, I'm sure. But one red flag needs mentioning. When you sense too much dependency from your child, or an anxiety-ridden relationship, take a hard look. You may be over-parenting and the offspring over-childing.

I doubt if we can change the dynamics of the old adage about always being a parent. But for healthy parent-child relationships we can (must) control it.

Loosening
the
Line
College

Loosening the Line
(College)

Caps 'n Gowns 'n Congrats

"Which side does my tassel go on?" smiling young women and men, outfitted in bigger-than-life caps 'n gowns, ask of their graduating neighbors and faculty. (And most of us can't remember.)

It's exciting, this business of graduating! Goals reached, dreams realized, pursuits achieved, new doors opening, suns rising, life calling, and tons of work and thousands of study-hours all behind.

And it's sad! Something breaking and many somethings ending. Friends leaving, old gangs breaking up, and watery eyes blurring vision, trying to hold back the clock.

Friendships, nurtured by years of mutual study and common tears over not-expected grades, are writing their last lines on the chalkboard just as Time takes eraser in hand and makes big strokes, reducing to white dust chapters that took years to write.

Friendships, built from the bricks and mortar of victories and defeats, laughter and weeping, joy and sorrow, seem destined for oblivion as classmates line up for final roll check.

Memory churns, focusing on past portraits, almost lifesize: parties, secrets, young loves borning, new values emerging, old securities abandoned, new ones embraced. And a whole era of the familiar suddenly replaced by the unknown, the unfamiliar, and the scary.

And these big gowns or robes? So bulky, so unfamiliar, belonging to another time. Why so big? I really don't know but I have my own theory.

Your graduate's gown is oversized because many, many people belong in that robe with you. Your parents, family, scores of teachers who have nourished and nurtured you into and through life belong there with you. You would not be who you are and what you are had they not loved, taught, and sacrificed for you.

John Donne was wrong when he said that "No man is an island." Fact is, every person is an island. Donne would have been right (and this is his real meaning, no doubt) had he said, "No person can remain an island."

We become islands when separated from mother-womb. And we spend our lives building bridges from our islands to other islands.

And tears at graduation (both sad and joyful tears) are liquid testimony that you have successfully built some bridges to other islands, and the bulky robe is mute witness to the fact that many people have given you bridge-building materials.

Congratulations to you and everybody inside your robe!

For Whom the (School) Bell Tolls

(To my friend Joe Legion, upon the occasion of his oldest daughter's matriculation as a college freshman — oops, freshwom . . . uh . . . uh . . . first-year college student! Whew!)

Dear Joe,

I know, I really know, what you're going through. This is your first. Last year I sat where you sit.

She is excited. You're not. She has been packing all summer. The little things she held in common with the rest of the family she must now have for herself — toothpaste, hairdryer, coffee-maker, shampoo, dictionary, soup-maker, tennis balls. There's something scary and final when they start getting their own things that once spelled family ownership.

You'll load up the station wagon and the whole family will squeeze in for the trip. The big family dog stands with his nose against the screen door, looking rejected and whimpering as lonely as you feel. Your sagging car's bumper makes a harsh but chilling kind of lonely sound scrapping its way out of the drive onto the street that leads her "way, way from home."

The whole family makes light talk and tries jokes on the way down. But the closer you get to that institution which will separate you from your first born — sometimes in a jerky, tearing surgical procedure — the conversation slows down.

43

You will pull the loaded wagon into a much-too-small space along with other parents who laugh and joke to mask their real feelings. They're all there it seems — the forty-crowd who entered college in the late forties and early fifties — standing there wondering where all the years have gone.

She makes quick friends with laughing girls in the hall. You leave them for a while and just stroll about the campus. You look at your wife. You remember. You both remember. You're remembering twenty-five years ago when the two of you, with the dew of youth bathing your faces, were ushered into that new and different world of college.

You know that it's so different now. More pressures, more to learn, more freedom; but you know also she will have to struggle with age-old challenges that have not changed — love, courtship, learning to belong, finding her place, finding herself, searching for her role in life.

You'll hold the tears, Joe, until you've headed the car away from her. Then they'll come. Let 'em come. They are the interest you pay on the loan of a daughter God gave you to love, teach and send into life with values to live life. Trust your teaching. You will find, and she will, too, that you did better than you think.

As the tears blur your vision of the winding road back home, you will know that you have entered a new era. Something has died! But something is being born. Nothing new can be born until something old has died. It is in dying that new life can be born.

She's on her own now. New doors will open. New relationships established. She'll make some mistakes. She'll hurt; pain will come, but truth and freedom lie somewhere beyond pain. There can be no real growth without pain; no maturity without hurt. Trust the process. Freedom will bring healing.

You will lose a daughter but you will gain a woman, and ultimately, a son — a man whom she will one day compliment by saying, "I do." And that will be a compliment to you. She will be saying, "Dad, I like men. You taught me by being a man, a father, that men are OK." And she'll turn to a man because you have given men a good reputation.

But now, Joe, it's not easy. Her room is empty and twice as big. And you'll look at it every night for awhile and with great emotion,' "Why? Why does it hurt so? Why does it have to be this way?"

And the answer, Joe, is: "When we love, we hurt. When we love, we let them go." That won't help your hurting. Nothing will.

But it's comforting to know, as you turn over for sleep, that she is God's child, too — and in His hands.

Your fellow hurting father

To Bridgette, Co-Ed

Dear Bridgette:

College is exciting. And college kids are excitement. Learning. Growing. Horizons expanding. Everything in present tense. Few nouns, mostly verbs. Lots of adjectives. Modifying what? Who?

Action. Nothing static, not much nailed down. Pulsating. Flitting and flirting. Fickled as a fumbled football. Dependable. Dependent. Searching for interdependence, and what it means.

Bumping new ideas. Being bumped hard for old ones, and traditions. Kidded for virginity. Absolutes questioned absolutely. Relativity enthroned. Black and white turned gray. Grayness getting foggy.

High roads and low roads, and in between misty flats where they drift to and fro. Learned "no man is an island," learning "every man is an island." Discovering the bridge-building business between, among islands.

Building bridges from learned to what's to be learned; building bridges from the old to the new; building bridges from home to a-home-away-from-home to a home-of-their-own-someday.

Experimenting. Failing. Succeeding. Faithing. Doubting. Finding more faith in honest doubt than creeds. Bridge-ing. Trying to bridge-it.

Bridgette is a co-ed. No one's daughter. Everyone's daughter. Trying to build her bridges; trying to bridge-it. Sometimes succeeding. Sometimes not. But searching; looking; hoping.

She becomes part of your life, your concern, your challenge.

She's trying to bridge-it between her parents' expectations of her and what she's able to accomplish.

Bridgette, it's not easy living up to another's expectations of you. Like David trying to do his thing in Saul's armor. Had to shed it and use his own uniform. Wasn't much better. Little old loin cloth and a slingshot. But it was his. And he did the job. Remember?

Reminds me what a college student said years ago. "Our greatest liability is our potential." Whew! That's heavy. But real. Our greatest burden sometimes is that which we could be. Privilege lays heavy responsibilities on us. Gifts ... talents ... IQ's. They demand production; big interest payments on investments; God's and other's.

Yet, high expectations motivate us. Low expectations devastate. High expectations say we are respected, held in high esteem, approved, and loved. Makes you feel good to know somebody thinks you've got what it takes.

The other day I saw a mother bird push a baby from the nest. Old bluejay. She hollered, screamed, cajoled so loudly I almost tried to fly! On the limb above her baby, she hollered. On the ground in front of him, she hollered. Finally, her baby-grown-big decided to try the two burdens on his back. He lifted them, stretched, and with her still hollering, started to fly! Guess he discovered his burdens were wings. Think maybe her expectations (high) sorta caused him to fly (high).

Think maybe that's the way it is, Bridgette. High expectations cause high achievement; low expectations, oh, well, you know.

Depends on whether you use them as BURDENS or WINGS. Have a good flight ... journey ... pilgrimage.

To Bridgette on Building

Dear Bridgette:

Everything nailed down is coming loose, huh? Guess it seems that way. At times, anyhow. Your last letter reminded me of what happened some years ago in the mountains of our state.

The county courthouse was about to fall down. Hadn't been repaired in years. The people were getting irritated about it.

Finally they prevailed on the grand jury to take a look at it.

They did. Then passed three resolutions. First, the courthouse should be torn down. Second, a new courthouse would be built with material from the old. Third, they should continue using the old while the new was being built!

I don't know how they accomplished that feat. Took some doing. Some kind of miracle. Yet, that's somewhat your situation during college years.

You are involved in building a new life, a new person. To be sure, you will use much of the material from the old life to build the new, and you will continue using the old while the new is being built.

Sounds hard. It is. But that's really the way it is. And it doesn't stop with college. It's a process that continues until death. And the moment it stops, you die. Oh, you may live on twenty-five more years before you're buried, but the moment you stop you die.

There are several ways you can approach this. You can simply tear down the old building and junk everything. Some do. Anything old is obsolete, they philosophize. But that doesn't make good sense. Use common sense about it. Horse sense, the old people called it. (By the way, horse sense requires stable thinking!)

Think with stability. Does it really make sense to junk all you've learned? You learned to add, subtract, etc. in grade school. You're a long way from that now. It's old stuff. But is it junk? Still use it, don't you? (Incidentally, try it on your bank stubs!)

I won't belabor the point. Just want to say that all old things (morals, religion, love, friendship) are not obsolete because they are old; and all new things are not progress simply because they are new.

Examine both. Investigate all. Nothing wrong with honest doubt, so long as it's honest. Honest doubt searches, examines, evaluates and decides. It's like brushing sand off the rock on which you stand. Once you get it off, your foundation is safer, more solid.

Questioning is not sin. But to accept without question is crime; crime against truth and yourself. That means questioning the NEW as well as the old.

47

Don't be afraid to examine your convictions. To have the courage of one's convictions means having the courage to take them out occasionally and examine them.

Truth will not melt under the bright light of investigation. God will not crumble with the weight of questions or doubts. He can take it. He invites searching. His Son said on one occasion: "Seek and you shall find . . ."

How our friends in the mountains accomplished their task, I don't know. But I know you will. You'll build a new temple of life with material from the old, and you'll continue using the old while you build the new.

Happy building, good searching, and enjoy it. You'll be doing it the rest of your life!

A Myth, Bridgette, A Myth

Dear Bridgette,

Your letter dealt with a real issue alive on campuses and in communities. "Living in," or "Living together without benefit of marriage," is becoming so commonplace it's hardly up for discussion. Or so I'm told. But I must contend it's still up for discussion. Until all evidences and data are in, it's still open for discussion. (The emotional, psychological, mental and spiritual effects have yet to be conclusively examined.)

Your discussion group asked that I not refer to the moral and ethical teaching of the Bible as a basis for authority. I'll have some difficulty at that point. You see, the Bible (among other things) is a record of what people have discovered will and will not work. Its moral teachings are discoveries of the way God put us together. God gives moral principles, not to prohibit our freedom, but to grant it.

When I was a lad Dad built a play-car for me. He said it had direct-ratio steering. (Turn the steering wheel one inch and the front wheels turned one inch.) He told me to be careful when I turned the steering wheel or it would cut so sharply I'd end up in the ditch. (I did several times!) He gave that basic principle, not to limit my freedom, but to expand it. That was the way the car was made.

The Bible simply tells us how we're put together, who put us together, and why. It says we're made — man and woman — to live together, to become family (even if no children come) and be a contributing couple to the community. And this family-ness happens on the basis of commitment; a commitment of two people to love (and nurture love) in the framework and context of marriage.

Now, Bridgette, there are two myths used to justify "living in" or "living together without marriage."

First, love produces marriage. Myth one. It's the other-way-round. Marriage produces love. (A certain degree of love launches marriage, but once launched, marriage produces love.) Marriage is produced by fidelity, and fidelity becomes possible only by commitment. Marriage is a contract based on fidelity. Without commitment, fidelity is impossible. Living together without marriage has no long-term commitment. And commitment is the first step in creating love; a love that can generate fulfillment each heart longs for.

Myth two: if two people live together for a period of time (two years, let's say) they can determine if they can make it the rest of their lives. That philosophy assumes the two people would not change after the so-called "trial period." It assumes you learn everything about a person in two years; that a person (and relationship) becomes static; nobody grows; everything is nailed down and further change is impossible. The untruth of that myth needs no further comment.

The great ethical and moral teachers of history advocate marriage, family, home, not to prohibit life, but to provide it. Their teachings come not so much from theory as discovery; a discovery of what will work and what won't.

Moral and ethical roots are important, not just for a coat-of-arms, but arming us for the future in light of what has been discovered. And what will work.

Un-mythically yours

P.S. Incidentally, Webster defines MYTH as "an ill-founded belief held uncritically especially by an interested group."

On Screaming

Recently I read about a nightly incident that takes place at eleven o'clock on the campus of Cornell University. They call it The Primal Scream. Hundreds of students throw open their windows and scream for ten minutes.

It's loudest during exams. Other colleges have taken negative note of it, almost to the embarrassment of Cornell's dean who admits it goes on but wishes that "many other activities" would be cited.

Well, Dean, I'm not so sure that your reaction should be all that negative. (Maybe he's forgotten the tension that builds up during the semester, especially exam time.)

Sometimes a good, loud scream does more for the mind and soul than almost anything else. And it might prevent more drastic actions on the part of students.

I have often felt that a blood-curdling yell might get the old blood flowing again, resulting in positive actions that come from the insides being at peace once again.

And I'm sure that some faculty and college administrators feel like a good scream, especially during those days when higher education is getting higher all the time, and money to operate is getting harder and harder to come by.

Parents come in high on the schedule of persons needing to scream. And that's not a bad idea. (Fact is, at times I've wanted to scream in their behalf!)

But a word of caution to parents. If and when you scream, take the Cornell students' procedure as example — stick your head out the window, not in the faces of your children (or spouse).

The unwritten law of screaming is this: You do it to the outdoors, not to people. They may think you are upset with them rather than at yourself.

Screaming (out-a-window, out-of-doors) may become a time-honored method of relieving whatever has you uptight. And we may see academic courses offered in Screamology; time-management in industry may be replaced with scream-management, and stadiums filled as communities come together to practice screaming. All people and professions may become involved.

Wonder which window would be the best?

The Cost

The sign announced that a college group would have a seminar on, "The Cost of Growing Up."

As I wandered on down the hall looking for the coffee pot,

those words haunted, sticky-like. I mused that growing up does cost; man, how it costs.

But just as I turned toward the coffee urn with its aroma stimulating my caffeine withdrawal symptoms, something surfaced in my mind even more haunting and sticky than the cost of growing up.

How about "The Cost of NOT Growing Up?" Man, there's a question that not only haunts; it scares you to death.

As I put the coffee pot back on the warm burner, I put that scary question on the front burner. It's not boiled or cooked even yet, but here are some of the smells coming from the almost-boiling pot.

The cost of NOT GROWING UP:

Means you continue to tear your britches on the same nail, never learning from past mistakes or past successes.

Means you think you must invent the wheel again, never learning from others or using their experiences as guides over life's bumps.

Means you never get off the ground, constantly taxiing up and down the same runway, missing the beauty of the world just waiting for your discovery.

Means you die before you ever live, even though your funeral is forty years down the road.

Means you never know reality, always waiting for something bigger and better to turn up, hoping that life will thus turn into something big and beautiful for you.

Means you will search under every stone and behind every tree for happiness but will never find it. Because it is not only within you; it is you.

Means you will never know freedom because the chains of immaturity will make you its prisoner, ripping from you the liberty you were created to enjoy.

Means you will be a slave to whatever is easy, safe, and requires little or no effort. Risk will not be in your vocabulary nor in your attempts.

The cost of growing up is expensive, but the cost of not growing up promises bankruptcy.

The Emptiness of an Emptying Nest

She's your youngest, the last of what once had been a triangle of three. You watch as she packs her belongings, then with indecision puts them back with the explanation, "I won't need this until cold weather."

Standing before an array of cosmetics, haircurlers, and all those do-dads of feminine scaffolding, you watch her pick-and-choose, wondering how in heaven's name she'll ever get it all into her little car!

You stand by helplessly, watching as her mother does all those mother-things that only mothers do, and you ponder what you could do, maybe ought to be doing.

You think perhaps a book from you might help. You busy yourself writing an inscription on the flyleaf, fighting back tears as you write, realizing what challenge, joy, life, and love the youngest one has brought to your life.

The car is finally loaded, and you mean loaded! Clothes, books, and the hundred-and-one things little girls accumulate over the years and declare necessities, cause the car to swing low to the concrete which you know will bump the bumper when she pulls out of the driveway — and it does.

Then you see the big teddy bear perched on top of the clothes in the back seat, and you smile. The tug the teddy bear makes on your heart also signals that there may be a woman at the wheel in the front seat, but in the back seat — and behind all the woman-ness — there is still part of that little girl who used to snuggle in your lap like a live teddy bear. And you're glad, and you hope that part of "that little girl" will live on and on and on.

The final picture is shuttered with your camera. You and her mother stand helpless, watching her maneuver the car (that has been passed-down the family three times) out of the driveway into the street. There's the final wave, and the first tear. You've been holding that tear because she asked you the night before to "please don't cry until I'm gone."

Back in the empty house you walk to three empty bedrooms, looking at three smiling faces on photograph paper. And for the first time in your life you know the gut-feelings of the famous (infamous?) "Empty Nest Syndrome." And you're hurting.

Somehow her Persian cat senses the LOSS, and curls in a furry ball on the floor when normally he would have been out doing whatever it is cats do on a cool, fall-approaching morning.

And the family German Shepherd seems to feel your grief, and parks himself in docile fashion at your feet while you mobilize grief on your typewriter, sharing your feelings with thousands of known and unknown readers who somehow will KNOW and understand the emptiness a father feels when he first touches the prickly edges of the empty-nest.

When They All Leave

"What's it like when all the children have left home?" I have asked that question over the years while we still had three little ones pitter-pattering through the house with leaden feet.

But now I know! It's different, to say the least. First, there's a stillness that's almost morbid. The deafening "sounds of silence" create all sorts of noises: like, "I thought I heard her voice," or, the imagination of loud rock music emitting through the heating system as in days past.

Then there's the sudden realization that when you put something down it will be there when you go back. My nail clippers, for instance. They never were where I left them. But today I picked them up where they have been resting for nearly a week. I wanted to shout, "Why don't you move? Get lost, like you used to!" They just sit there, staring back in frustrated silence, wondering also why I can find them so easily.

And my throw-away razor never moves from where I put it. Fact is, I thought it was an automatic throw-away invention — it always seemed to disappear when about half-gone, or half-dull. Now it just stays there, always available when I reach for it. Sometimes I hide it from myself to get old feelings to kick-up.

There's my dictionary right where it's supposed to be. How many times I've reached for it, only to get a handful of air and give the household an air full of my wrath for causing me to lose my train of thought while looking for Mr. Webster.

And out in my workshop tools stay disgustingly where I

drop them. Always thought the kids caused workshop disorganization, but that myth has been exploded. (The Better-Half pointed that out. The other day — just to make me feel good, I think — she put my favorite hammer in her utility room. "There's my hammer," I exploded. She smiled knowingly, and I put it back where she had left it, just to preserve a touch of the past.) I'll holler for it sometime soon (when I'm holding two pieces of lumber together, and a poised nail in a half-full hand). The hollering will be more of a CALL for the past — it won't do any good, but I'll feel better!

Their mother looks across the table at their father, and their father looks back at their mother. And both realize that father-mother roles are diminishing as the little-ones-now-adults find their ways in the world.

So the husband-wife roles take on new and different meanings, but every now and then the father-mother roles emerge, and a few silent tears trickle to mark the passing of an era that is gone, but will never be forgotten.

Lengthening
the
Line

Aging

Lengthening the Line
(Aging)
The Glory of Grandparenting

I'm not a grandparent, but someday I look forward to the experience, and privilege. So what I say comes from the perspective of an observer, and a recipient of excited grandparents extolling the virtues of their grandest-ones, complete with visual aids of recently taken pictures, in-focus and out-of-focus.

Don't get me wrong. I'm not being critical. Fact is, I support so completely grandparents' "inherent right" to give their grandchildren high visibility that I designed an "official grandparents' license" they can carry with them to make legal their tendency to brag.

The license boldly states that "Whereas John Doe is now a Grandparent it is his inalienable right to exaggerate the fine qualities of his grandchildren, and minimize their weaknesses and faults. Furthermore, he is now privileged to show their pictures on every possible occasion, and otherwise enjoy the pleasant role of grandparenthood."

A friend of mine said, "Had I known grandchildren could be so wonderful I would have had them first!" How's that for a grandparental testimony? I don't know how he would have accomplished that feat, but the idea appeals to many experienced people.

Another friend states that "grandparents are either lonely or exhausted." We're probably getting down to basic truth with that candid confession. He explains that when the grandchildren are not visiting him, he is lonely. Wants to see them; be with them.

"But," he admits, "it's amazing how quickly you can catch-up and fulfill all your past loneliness when they arrive for a visit."

"Grandchildren are exhausting," my friend confides. "I

56

know why God gives children to you when you are young — you can't take too much of their demands when you hit your fifties and sixties."

I used to think how happy our children's grandparents must have been when they saw us coming for a long visit. Now I have a sneaking suspicion they were not nearly as overjoyed with our three bouncing kids as I thought, especially after we had been there a few days.

Although I'm not a grandparent, I'm approaching that mental and physical age that enables me to appreciate the fact that grandparents are either lonely or exhausted. (I wouldn't write this were I a grandparent, and I'll deny authorship when that glorious grandparenting day comes!)

But suffice it to say, grandparents do have their limits, and those limits are more confined than we often realize. So, my fellow parents of the world's greatest grandchildren, let's strike a good balance between loneliness and exhaustion for the grandparents. O.K.? Good!

Age Is In The Mind of The Beholder

His name was William. But he liked for me to call him Willie. He became my administrative assistant on a church staff when he was seventy-five. He had retired as postmaster years before. A good administrator. Liked details and loved people. Visited in the hospitals every day and kept the wheels of a big church running smoothly.

Willie had been on the staff three years when he traded cars. One Sunday morning — as he made his way to church to check out everything before the congregation arrived — a man ran a stop light and bumped Willie's new car.

The next morning he moaned to me about the slight accident that had wrinkled a rear fender.

"Who did it?" I asked.

"Some old man," Willie answered. "Didn't look where he was going."

"How old is he?" I pushed the issue.

Willie broke out in a sheepish grin.

"'Bout fifty-nine or sixty-nine."

We both rolled with laughter, and the ageless Willie at

seventy-eight laughed the loudest.

Age is in the mind of the beholder. Willie never thought of himself as being old. Old age was something that happened to other people, never to him.

The last time I saw Willie he was over eighty-five and going strong. He talked of the future as if he plans to be there. And he will. His sense of humor is as keen as ever. He knows how to laugh; he likes to laugh.

It occurs to me even as I write this I've just given some guidelines for staying young. Think young. Old age is something that happens to other people, not you. Think of the future as a personal appointment; plan to be there. And, above all, keep that sense of humor.

Willie is a writer, a poet in his own right. He'd probably re-write Browning's famous verse:

Come, grow (not old) just GROW
Along with me.
The best is NOW — we'll handle the 'yet-to-be'
By now-ing ourselves into the future.

Well, I owe apologies now to Willie and Browning. But I know Willie will understand, and knowing Browning through his verses, think he would, too.

I'd like to "go along and grow" with both of them.

Never Know When You'll Need It!

He was eighty. Both feet turned in until his toes met. Walked with two canes, but could out-walk most teenagers. Loved life and everybody. Everybody loved Mr. Joe, as he was affectionately called in the small town.

One day he banged on my office door and burst in, all at the same time.

"Have you got a typing book I could borrow?" he asked with a sense of urgency.

"A what?"

"A typing book. You know, a book you learn how to type from."

"No," I told him. "You can probably get one over at the high school."

"Would you call over there for me and ask?"

"Yes," I promised. "But may I ask what you want with a typing book?"

"I want to learn how to type."

I sat amazed. I looked at him closely. Eighty years old with fingers that reflected all eighty years. I dialed. Yes, they would loan him one.

He started to leave.

"Mr. Joe, why do you want to learn to type?" I asked as tactfully as I could.

"You just never know when you'll need it," he answered in all candor as he breezed out the door toward the high school.

Six months later a small pulp-wood company opened an office in town. They needed someone to answer the phone and do some typing.

Mr. Joe got the job! At eighty.

He never stopped growing. I was still in my twenties when Mr. Joe gave me a basic philosophy on preparedness: "You never know when you'll need it."

And you never do. No experience or preparation is ever wasted unless we allow it. Opportunity comes to those who are prepared for the visit.

I never cease to be amazed how young some old people are. Aging may take its toll on people in direct proportion to how well they have prepared themselves to keep growing and learning and living.

Old age may hit the moment a person stops dreaming. "You never know when you'll need it." That could be one principle to keep old age from happening. Who knows?

As Long As You Plan

There may be more truth than poetry in this statement: we live about as long as we plan to. Could be when people stop planning they don't live long thereafter.

A case in point, maybe. Seventeen years ago I met James Larkin Pearson, poet-laureate of North Carolina. He had just moved back to his native town. We became good friends.

One day he was showing me his study with its nearly five thousand books. In a room adjoining his study was an old hand-operated printing press on which he had turned out thousands of printed words. All the scaffolding and artifacts of a writer leaned against the walls of the newly constructed study waiting for the hand and mind of the creator to use them for communication of thoughts too deep for tears, but surfacing just enough for a poet's apt use.

"I have planned my work for the next twenty years," he told me with a voice strong for its eighty years. He noticed my somewhat startled look which efforts at concealment had failed to hide.

"I'm serious," he said seriously to his new-found friend and could-be-skeptic. "I have it all planned out. And I plan to see my plans fulfilled."

Eleven years later — at 91 — he published a major compilation of his poetry. Recently I joined his many friends at a community college where he celebrated his 97th birthday.

He looked as well as the first day I met him, maybe better. His dress was up-to-date. Even his graying hair sported a new style, blown-dry and all!

He might just make it — his twenty-year plan. Only three years short. And, knowing the poet, he's revised his plan and has extended it beyond his 100th milestone.

Who's to say. His plan — and all that goes into making it work — may be largely responsible for his long life.

We may live just about as long as we plan to. When we no longer plan — no longer look forward to the future — we are already dead. We may not be buried yet, but we are dead.

The most devastating situation is to arrive at the end of one's roadmap. A person's in trouble when that happens.

There's an old saying, has a lot of truth in it: "Plan your work and work your plan." It may lengthen your life. Even if it doesn't, it gives the time left meaning and purpose and fun.

We live about as long as we plan to. Could be true. Think I'll plan like it is anyhow.

Destination: Rest Home

"We are torn up," they often begin. "Time has come to put mother in a rest home. We've tried everything. She can't live alone and none of the children has room. All of us work. She'd still have a home if we could keep her."

Guilt, grief, trauma — written all over their faces. The most difficult experience any family faces. And scores of families are facing the situation every day.

There are no easy answers for families at such times. The matter of safety for the aging parents becomes a primary concern and responsibility. Economically, families cannot afford parent-sitters while they are out of the home working. And, too, where do you find people who can live-in or parent-sit during the day? That's a dwindling profession.

Children often spend the rest of their lives feeling guilty over having placed their aging parents in rest homes. When they go visit them they are depressed by the fact parents are confined to a building with other aging parents.

But one thing we need to remember: while we would be bored, depressed and isolated if confined to a rest home at our age (forties and fifties), parents do not have many of the needs they once had when our age.

I'd be bored stiff if I had to spend my days in the first grade (or tenth grade, for that matter). When I was that age I was not bored. I liked it. Loved it. I had needs that were met at that age level. But I've passed out of that level.

By the same token, I've not reached the age or level of the rest home. I'm not ready yet. Too much energy. Too many worlds to conquer.

I have a feeling — though I cannot speak from experience — that aging parents feel at home among others of their same age group, like high school kids feel about their peer group. And I doubt, even in fantasy moments, I'd ever want to go back to high school age.

Could be aging parents — with energy level low and their world somewhat confined — would not want to return to my age level again. They may not be as happy as they were when they had their own homes and could go and come as they liked. But they may find a contentment among their own peer group in a structured life that gives security by offering safety.

I don't really know about it, not yet. Just some ideas. When I reach that age I may come back and tear up this writing, at least re-write it and say the fiftyish guy who wrote it ought to go soak his head.

And if I can make it down the hall of my rest home, I'll do it. And apologize for mis-reading the situation.

The
Line
Snaps
Death

The Line Snaps
(Death)
To My Son

My Dear, Dear Son,

The hundreds of friends and scores of relatives who flooded our home for the past few days have returned to their daily run of duty. I sit alone in your room, the place where you and I have spent many, many hours talking, discussing, raising more questions than we ever found answers for.

All the scaffolding of your short seventeen years stands in deafening silence — the catcher's mitt, bulletin board laden with girls' pictures, homecoming ribbons, stubs of special college football tickets, and a few momentos you never told me just what significance they held locked in their mute grasp.

Your drums that often rocked the house (and neighborhood) stand silent, never again to feel the rhythm of your body and soul. Wrinkled basketball shoes, a student council T-shirt with "President" stenciled on the back, a calendar stuffed with never-to-be-filled activities, rough drafts of term papers, an unfinished college application blank, and assorted books lie much as you left them on your desk.

A well-worn and daily-read Bible lies beside your bed, in easy reach. And a German Shepherd named Deacon roams frustratedly in and out of your room, often pausing to lie on the foot of your bed, wondering why you and I have not had any long night conversations there recently.

Son, you were doing something you loved — water skiing — when it happened. Of course, by now you know the whole story, and understand more about everything than we ever will. We still wander in the wordless silence of questioning spirits, trying to make sense of it all.

You touched so many lives in your short lifetime, more than most of us will ever touch in three-score and ten. In your life you touched hundreds; in your death you are touching thousands.

Yes, we are still asking WHY. Why did this happen? Why did it happen to you? Perhaps we'll never know the answer. Your mother, your sisters and I continue to ask this question with tears running unashamedly down our faces.

We are seeing many people's lives being changed through all this. And we are grateful. But in all honesty, our one desire is to have you back like you were — full of life, loving everybody you ever met, giving encouragement to people, dreaming dreams, making things happen, wrestling with me, getting ready for a date, washing the car, filling the rec room downstairs with guys under the pretense of studying chemistry (never knew chemistry to be that laugh-producing) and stuffing yourself with so-called snacks that were in fact major meals! (Mom loved that.) We miss all that, and you, son.

You and I discussed many questions during these past few years. Now you can find answers to them all. You beat me to it. I hope the first person you look up (after you experience the glory of standing face-to-face with God) is the Apostle Paul. He left a lot of questions dangling. You remember some of them, don't you? Ask him to clear them up.

Then go find Simon Peter, that lovable, impulsive fellow who tried everything, accomplished some, but in his attempts endeared himself to all who have ever slipped and fallen in their faith. You won't have much trouble recognizing him — you've lived in the same house with a guy like him for the past seventeen years!

Forest, we miss you. Our lives will never be the same again. We've learned a lot during these weeks about ourselves. And we've grown, matured.

I want to thank you for being the greatest son a father could ask for. I've never had to apologize for you or explain you. We have never worried or been concerned about you for a single moment. Somehow you got it all together early, and you had your head on straight. People congratulate your mother and me on being good parents. But, you know what? A good end in football makes the quarterback look great. Thanks for being a good end and making us look good.

You had just begun a course at school in Shakespeare. Soon

you would have found a statement in Julius Caesar that your
Dad feels describes you:

His life was gentle, and the elements
So mix'd in him that Nature might stand up,
and say to all the world,
 "This was a man!"

And your family? We are struggling, my Son, struggling.
Our faith has been tested to the core. The rafters of our
theology have trembled. We have touched the bottom, but I'm
happy to report to you that the bottom is solid! We shall make
it.

God keep you and God keep us all. We hurt, but we know
that to hurt deeply is to have loved deeply.

Loving deeply,
Dad, Mom, Becky, Rachel

God and Our Tragedies

Following our son's death, many questions surfaced, calling
into discussion God's participation in the tragic event.

Did God cause the accident? Was Forest's death God's will?
No mortal being can give definitive answers to such an age-old
question.

But I do have some theological beliefs and concepts that
have nurtured me as I have coped with our only son's death.

The first, and basic, belief is: "God did not cause this
tragedy!" We are free human beings, possessing the freedom
of choice. We choose what we want to do. And we live in a
world where accidents are possible, probable, and do happen.
Put freedom of choice and an accident-possible world together,
and you have potential tragedy.

Our son had an accident while doing something he loved.
Water skiing is dangerous, yes. But so is almost everything we
do. The only way to avoid such accidents is to take no risks in
life — and this would produce prisons where we would die of
physical, mental, emotional, and spiritual malnutrition.

God, who loves our son (and each of us), did not WILL, did
not desire, that his life be cut short after only seventeen years.
Yet, being free to live in a world where accidents can produce
death, our son met such an accident. God did not cause it; God

66

did not WILL it. It happened, accidentally.

However, God, in his love and wisdom, will not let this tragedy be wasted. He will — as He already has — step in and take this tragedy and bring good out of it. God has a way of taking shattered glass of broken dreams and making something new, something real, from the brokenness. Nothing in God's world is broken beyond some kind of repair.

One of our son's attending physicians wrote, asking if I (a minister) could explain why one so young died in such a tragic way.

My bottom-line answer was, NO! But I did share with him some of the ideas or theology about tragedy, none of which helped him, I'm sure. But I ended the letter, reminding him that theology which attempts to explain tragedy and suffering is somewhat like medicine given at the hospital to patients — medicine does not cure, at best it makes the patient more comfortable or re-enforces nature's healing process.

Theology which seeks to explain the inexplainable is little more than verbal medicine — it helps a little, makes us more comfortable perhaps, and maybe even re-enforce our faith until God and his Spirit of power, and his balm of time, can bring — not explanations — but healing and the ability to endure and cope.

A good friend and fellow minister brings it all into fine focus in the last paragraph of a letter to our family following the tragedy:

"God's participation at the point of cause may not be a good question for you and me to ask, but God's participation at the place of resolution, healing, strengthening is a good question and we can find God — not at the cause, but at the cure."

Except for the Limp

"We're doing a T.V. special on death and dying," she said over the phone. "Could we interview you on camera?"

When camera and lights had been set up, and all the entangling wires and plugs properly sorted out, the young, maturing T.V. personality started asking questions about the tangled wires and mis-matched plugs of death.

I could sense her hesitation in asking questions that would

kick up three-year-old emotions about the loss of our only son.

But I wanted to say, "You will not kick up anything new, because these emotions have been churning constantly since that day when a big part of our world crumbled."

"Do you ever get over the death of a loved one?" I've been asked that question many times. And my answer is still the same: "Not really!"

Oh, you take up the loose and tangled ends of your life and tie them together as best you can. You function as a person, but part of you died with that loved one, just as part of him lives with you.

A few months after Forest's (our son) death, a prominent pastor in a distant city lost his only son in an accident. I called my fellow minister to express concern and love.

With his Scottish accent he asked, "Do you ever get over this?"

I told him I didn't really know, but I doubted it. Maybe, I told him, it's like losing one of your legs in an accident. For weeks you suffer fresh wounds, totally incapacitated. But slowly healing happens. Crutches bridge the gap and shoulders of friends support, easing the pain of learning to walk again.

Soon an artificial leg is fitted. With proper therapy you learn to walk again, taking up the daily run of duty with much the same routine as before. Except for the limp.

But you never forget that at one time in your life you had two good legs. The limp won't let you forget. Nothing can make you forget.

You function much as before. Outwardly most people never know you are missing a leg. After a while even your close friends forget you lost a leg. Except for the limp.

And you never forget that at one time you had a son, that loved one. You function again. You live and laugh and love again. And outwardly most people may not know or remember.

Except for the limp.

Three Days Every Day

"Six months today," I heard myself say as I drove along the highway for an appointment. "Seems more like six hours," I muttered. But another part of me argued, "No, more like sixty years."

It had been six months (according to the calendar) since our only son died, victim of a freak accident on water skiis. But according to my feelings the time elapsed seemed somewhere between hours and years.

Why does grief produce such confusion of time, alternately making it seem only hours, then years? (And this is true whether the grief is produced by loss through death, divorce, or whatever.)

Time seems short and long because we actually live three days every day when we are in deep grief.

(1) We live each day "the way things were." Memory recalls how life used to be — the tender moments, the joys, the whole mix of experiences telescoped into each day. And the sharpness of memories, as warm and tender as they are, nevertheless produce a pain, a longing for what once was and can never be again. That hurts, and produces a vividness which prolongs the past, making it almost present, yet pushing it far away because time past cannot really be touched again.

(2) And we live each day "the way things are." Reality must become real — jobs to go to, other lives to touch, meals to cook, houses to clean, oil to change in the car, and dozens of other real things to do. Yet the doing of these reality-things jars memory of things-past and creates visions of what-might-have-been. And this kicks-up all sorts of feelings that prolong hours into days of suffering, confusing the passage of time until one wonders what is reality and what is not.

(3) Then we live each day "the way things could have been." This is the hardest, most difficult day of all. It is the day lived in the "Wilderness of IF," the "Valley of What-if," and on the lonely "Road of If-Only."

It is a day confused by fantasized dreams: we would have done this together; he would have liked this; we would have gone to that play and loved it; we would have done this . . . this . . . this; if, what if, if only . . .

And the days are sometimes like hours, sometimes like years, and sometimes like not anything. Because grief is a reality hard to grasp; makes it often so . . . so, unreal.

But the Great Physician lovingly anoints us with the healing salve of Time, and someday the three days will become only one. The past and future will not burden our present, but will become what they are — past and future — and give us warmness and reality by giving us perspective. (Not understanding, mind you, but perspective.)

Tip-Toeing Around Tragedy

Loss comes in all sizes, and every size brings grief. Death and divorce are perhaps the largest sizes of grief, certainly the most common and frequent. And to the person experiencing the losing, the loses are labeled tragedy.

What do you do when your friend experiences a tragic loss? Most of us can handle the initial response: we go to them, offer our sympathy, take a dish of food, send flowers (in death situations), and take the person out for dinner (in divorce ordeals).

But what do you do after a few days or weeks? Most of us run out of roadmap by then. The common complaint I hear from people grieving over death or divorce is: "Friends just tip-toe around my tragedy, never mentioning it or giving me a chance to talk about it. Their tip-toeing makes me angry, and it hurts!"

There are some Do's and Don'ts in dealing with your friend's loss:

Don't try to have business as usual with your friend; that is, don't ignore reality. The loss is real, so be real in your approach to it.

Do let the person talk about his loss. When he starts talking let him talk, ask strategic questions to help him keep talking. He will close the subject when he's through. Don't you try to close it! (There is therapy for him in talking about the tragedy. In a real sense you become a therapist by letting him talk.)

Don't dry his tears. Crying does not hurt; it releases hurt and brings healing. Don't give into the temptation and tendency to change the subject.

Do, from time to time, over the weeks following the tragedy, say to your friend such statements as: "Just want you to know I'm thinking about you." Or, "You are in my prayers." Maybe say, "I'm hurting with you." Your friend will, if he needs to, pick up on your offer and talk about his feelings.

Don't (unless you've been through a similar, and I mean similar, experience) ever say, "I know just how you feel." You

70

don't, not unless you have actually been there. Yet, somehow communicate your struggle to understand. "I don't know how you feel, not really, but it must be terrible!" Such a sentence will open all sorts of doors for your friend.

There are many "do's and don'ts" involved in relating to people in their grief. But there are two basic facts or guidelines to keep in mind:

1. Grief, if properly processed, lasts at least six to twelve months. During that time the hurt is fresh, like a wound. Healing and scar tissue begin to form after about a year.

2. Don't tip-toe around the person's tragedy. If you do, you become part of his problem. Be a part of the solution. Face the loss with the person, talk about it with him, and let him know you hurt with him. Please, for his sake, don't pretend nothing has happened! Be real, and face reality with him.

Seasoned
Lines

Special Days

Seasonal Lines
(Special Days)

Happy New . . . What?

Ah, a New Year! All un-spotted. Clean. Without blemish. It's a new slate, a clean sheet, we're told. You can begin again, we're encouraged.

But can we? For centuries poets, philosophers and would-be-seers of pulpit and pen have led us to believe that at the stroke of mid-night on December 31, something magical happens. Suddenly everything becomes new; all previous problems, contracts, plans are null-and-void. All bridges are burned. But is it so? Not really. We come into the new year with baggage that dates back many years, demanding our best efforts and energies.

We simply cannot entertain the idea that "everything is new." Commitments, both positive and negative, must be honored and dealt with. Life is more complex than a new calendar, no matter how clean its pages.

The Barn Baby of Bethlehem did not change the world by relieving people of former problems and responsibilities. (I have not come to destroy the law but fulfill it, said he.) What he did was give people new spirit, new life, to deal with old problems.

And so we come into the New Year, shackled by old problems, ideas, and lingering burdens. But we can approach them with a new spirit, born of new resolutions, mid-wived by revolutionary determination. The only thing NEW about The New Year is the spirit within us that will allow us to "make all things new" as we come to old things with new and re-birthed commitments.

Life is won or lost not by the circumstances we meet, but what the circumstances meet in us. The year is not new unless it meets a new You; and a new You can make every year —

every day — new.

Happy New You!

Easter

Easter is easily ruined. (For some people.) It happened to me when I was a little boy. It snowed on Easter! I was devastated because I could not wear my new white-linen suit, complete with short pants and black bow-tie.

I saw it almost happen recently to the children in our Child Care School. Creative teachers had designed a beautiful Easter Bunny outfit, put a willing teacher inside, and entertained the children. But when she took the suit off, it was left scattered about the room and the children saw it. The yell went up in unison, "Somebody's killed the Easter Bunny!"

Now that took a lot of explaining and counseling! Easter credibility hung on the ropes.

Easter was almost ruined for Jesus' disciples. The snow of unexpected events, the cross-winds of Calvary, the storm-tossed emptiness of a tomb that didn't make sense, plus the scattering of hopes around the room of faith, had combined to extend the blackness of Friday and Saturday to cover not only Sunday but all Sundays ahead.

But something happened. And Easter exploded in them. It started when the scriptures started making sense. The resurrected Christ was walking with two disciples who had not recognized him. Jesus said, "O foolish men, and slow of heart to believe all the prophets have spoken. (Lk. 24:25) Then Luke says: "And beginning with Moses and all the prophets, he interpreted to them in all the scriptures, the things concerning himself." (Lk. 24:27)

Easter exploded in them when the scriptures started making sense. Jesus took the events of Easter, focused their thinking on yesterday's facts of prophecy, then pointed them to the future with meaning. When we come to know the WHY of Easter; the WHY of Good Friday and Black Saturday; the WHY of discipleship, then we can put up with almost any HOW, and any circumstance, situation, or problem. It is Easter! The WHY is answered with the shout: "He is risen!"

75

Mother's Day

Mother's Day. It kicks up all sorts of memories, images, and nostalgia. It is a day "dedicated to the memory of the best mother in the world, your mother," so stated the U.S. Congress on May 10, 1913 as they designated the second Sunday in May as Mother's Day. The first proclamation of Mother's Day was issued by President Woodrow Wilson the following May.

Miss Anna M. Jarvis, a native of Grafton, WV, birthed the idea of a special day for mothers as early as 1907 in memory of her own beloved mother. The custom became a national tradition in the U.S.A. and later spread to Latin America and the Orient.

Mother. It's a special word that puts us in touch with our earliest memories. It speaks of love, care, discipline and a host of experiences that spell life. Sadly, for some people, negatives surface and prick old wounds with sharp needles of it-never-was-good-for-me.

But perhaps all of us have experienced "Mother" and "mothering" from some person who functioned in that role for us. She may have been grandmother, aunt, step-mother or some other person who loved with mother-love and rightly deserves title and respect of mother.

I was lucky. I had two mothers — my mother and grandmother. These two women touched my life differently and in many ways. For some time during my teenage years it bothered me that I felt deeply for BOTH mothers, like maybe disloyalty of affection for my mother.

· But a wise counselor reminded me that what was happening in my life was what is now called "extended family." The love and relationship with both women complimented rather than diminished the role of each in my experience. (Some in my family would say that the love of these two women served to spoil me doubly! I refuse to comment on that.)

Mothers are human beings. None is perfect, but each has a special and unique dimension without which no civilization could happen nor survive.

Mothers have the uncanny ability to know our needs even before we invent them. They have ability to detect thoughts before we think them, pitfalls before they're there, and cliffs before we walk off them.

Mother has the hands of a craft without being crafty; the nose of a news reporter without being nosy (most of the time); she has the insight of a prophet without profit (at our expense); but most of all, she has a heart of love, merely another way to spell MOTHER.

Reflections

"Mother" is a word that churns up all sorts of feelings, images, and loves. And when you take a phone call the day after Christmas from a physician 300 miles away saying, "I'm sorry, but your mother just died," something deep inside goes numb — and something inside you dies.

For fifty years when you said, spoke, or called, "Mother," she answered.

You remember the little things — and the big ones. The first birthday party; the skinned knee kissed well; the protection from dragons in your bedroom at night, brushed away by a touch and kiss.

And you remember the first day of school and you wondered why she cried; and when you stumbled over furniture in the dark during high school days trying to slip in an hour beyond curfew only to have her call, "Is that you?" and you wanted to say No.

Then when you left for college you again saw her tears; and when the family car rolled off campus, and you got alone, you cried, too — this time understanding more about her tears.

You remember the pride on her face each time a diploma or degree was bestowed upon you; and the letters, gifts, and care-packages of goodies arriving during those bachelorhood days.

And the joy at your wedding and her thrill the three times you called about her being a grandmother; and the deep hurt she felt and showed at the grave of her eldest grandson.

Then with hurt you saw disease cripple her until you could carry her eighty pounds comfortably in your arms; and when the end came you knew her body, not death, was her enemy.

Something deep inside stirred as you drove back home and you decided you would help conduct her funeral service. When you stood in the pulpit of the church where your family (both sides of the tree) have worshipped for generations, you faced your aging father and relatives and felt a Presence from outside yourself giving strength as you shared personal thoughts about one whose life gave you life and the word "Mother" slipped from present tense to past.

"Thank you" and "Mother" — words that say it all, needing no commentary.

My Dad

There's a special relationship between father and son, and when word comes that father has died suddenly (six weeks short of 85), all sorts of emotions flood your soul.

Snapshots of your half-century-plus experiences with him come into sharp focus as you drive the hundreds of miles to take charge of arrangements and ultimately stand in the family home church and help conduct his funeral, making good on a promise to him of many years' vintage.

Dad was a lumberman; emphasis on both LUMBER and MAN. He loved fine wood, especially black walnut. And with the skill of a master craftsman he created grandfather clocks, chests, and dozens of prized furniture pieces. He had the poet's feel for creative beauty; what the poet does with words, Dad did with wood.

He was a Man's Man. Standing nearly six feet, and carrying 200 pounds of hard muscle (in his prime), he commanded respect from those who worked for him and with him in his sawmill and furniture manufacturing days. (And this little boy, who often tagged along whenever permitted, felt a deep security under all sorts of circumstances.)

Dad became an active churchman during his middle years, having been a "bit slow in getting started," as he put it. He held practically ever office in the church except pastor, and he held the pastor's hand during difficult times of church-stress.

His heart condition prompted a five-months' stay in our home, some 300 miles from his beloved North Carolina homeplace. But one day during a long father-son talk he convinced me to take him home to live out his final years. His health had greatly improved.

From the moment he stepped into his home, he came alive. As the weeks wore on he became stronger: planted garden, mowed lawn, built furniture, and discovered lonely widows who needed taking out for dinner!

Then on a Sunday morning, having finished breakfast, he sat down in his favorite chair with his Sunday School book opened to the day's lesson. And his Call came immediately; no struggle, perhaps no warning. Thus ended the precious relationship I have cherished all my life.

But, oh, the snapshots I have etched in my mind and soul! They now become portraits of philosophy; paintings of theology; canvases of common sense, but most of all, framed pictures of love.

Thanks, Dad, for teaching me not only how to be a man, but how to be God's man.

Freedom Is Not A Piece of Paper

It was just a piece of paper, not much more. On it were written words — beautiful words, hot words, biting words. At first only two people signed it — the president and secretary of the group. Later fifty-three members signed it; even later four more completed the signing.

It was just a piece of paper. They called it the Declaration of Independence. It contained words that could spell death or could mean life to a new nation struggling for birth.

Its watchword was freedom, containing only one blindspot that refused to free all people as persons. It maintained the institution of slavery. Another eighty-five years would pass before Abraham Lincoln put a P.S. to it and proclaimed emancipation of slaves.

Just a piece of paper, but it launched a revolution the likes of which this world had never known, giving freedom to, of, for people who would live, fight, and die to keep freedom alive, not only from outside enemies but from inside friends who would step over the line toward tyranny.

Often it has been necessary to flash the sword at the front door in the face of invading strangers and also necessary to flush the kitchen sink near the backdoor of our American family whose misbehavior was not corrected by the milder discipline of soapy mouth-washings.

From the Halls of Montezuma to the top of Heart-Break Ridge and on to Saigon the sword has flashed, and back home the family sink has been flushed to rid the nation's honor of domestic and internal scandals, focusing on the Benedict Arnolds, Teapot Domes, and Watergates.

It all started with a piece of paper, but the parchment with the original signatures was permanently sealed in 1894 in a steel case to keep it from light and air. The document was illegible and almost faded following an attempt to have a copper-plate facsimile made in order to give copies to the signers and their heirs in 1823. The process ruined the original.

No one has laid eyes on the freedom document since 1894. But freedom is not a piece of paper!

It is an idea, a concept, a lifestyle, an experience, and — our forefathers believed — a right! The original Declaration of Independence has faded, but its ideas, concepts, and words are burned forever in the soul of this nation and etched on the hearts and minds of persons for whom life is liberty and for whom freedom is more precious than life itself.

And so may it ever be!

Something Missing

Her name was Beatrice, but friends had nicked it to Trixie. Tall, attractive with an engaging smile, she was about twenty-six. She boarded our bus just after it cleared Checkpoint Charlie and entered East Berlin, threading its way through the maze of walls and concrete barriers designed more to keep East Berliners in than the free world out.

Her English was flawless as she pointed out the various points of interest in the walled city. (We seemed to be going in circles of Communist showcased buildings and streets. We passed the same building four times by actual count.) But there was something missing in her tour-director smile, and sun glasses partially covered eyes that didn't sparkle but could have.

She was courteous, and there seemed to be a genuine interest in us as well as a sincerity in attempts to answer our questions.

But I was haunted by that indefinable "something" that was missing in a young woman about the age of our first-born.

What was it, I kept asking myself. When the bus stopped for picture-taking at the War Memorial where uniformed East Berlin honor guards marched in shades of the old Nazi goosestep, I had a chance to talk with her privately.

"We like you," I said smiling and with genuine feeling. "Our people would like to take you back with us," and I broadened the smile to defuse any fear on her part. She thanked me and said that she'd like that but wouldn't be able to.

"Have you ever been over to West Berlin?" I asked, getting serious.

She nodded No.

"Have you ever been out of your city?" I asked, steering clear of using "East Berlin," a term we'd been advised never to use over there.

"Oh, yes," she said. I have been to Russia and other socialist countries, but never to the West."

Perhaps she perceived from my silence the frustration I was feeling. She added quickly, "They may let me go over there not this year but next," and I detected excitement over that possibility.

When the tour was over, she rode with us back to Checkpoint Charlie but got off just before we entered the ordeal of being cleared for departure.

I looked back at her standing on the corner as she followed us with her eyes, waving goodbye.

Then I knew what that "something" missing in her smile and eyes was: FREEDOM. LIBERTY.

Flight 67 to Freedom

Pan American's flight No. 67 had hardly become airborn from Germany's Frankfurt airport when I became aware of a small group sitting to my left on the giant 747 headed for New York's Kennedy terminal some seven hours away.

There were five in the little group — a husband, wife, their ten-year-old daughter, and two men in their early fifties sitting immediately behind them. I soon determined that the father was the older brother of the two men, neither of whom could speak English. The father talked to his wife and daughter in English and to his brothers in a foreign language.

For several hours I watched as the older brother did all sorts of special things for them — getting extra drinks, food, and small souvenirs from airline attendants. He was extremely attentive to them, and seemed delighted he could do special things for them.

After a few hours of watching this drama of celebration, my curiosity got the better of me. I approached the man, apologized for my curiosity, and asked if they were his brothers.

"Yes," he said, smiling and shared with me what was happening.

"Twenty-eight years ago I escaped from my home in Czechoslovakia and found freedom and career in California. When I escaped they put my brother in prison and sent him to a work camp in the coal mines. During that time he lost his left arm.

"I made a promise to myself and my parents that one day I'd come back and take my brothers, who have suffered under Communism, to America, at least for a long visit. For the past two years I have worked through Communist red-tape for the privilege of taking them to America for three months.

"They have never been in a free country. When we landed in Frankfurt this morning, they breathed free air for the first time. It nearly blew their minds! Everything is a "first" for them — the airplane flight, the stores filled with goods, enough food to eat, and no one watching over their shoulders."

When we touched down in New York the 400-plus passengers applauded our safe arrival, but those two brothers applauded louder and longer than any of us. Their smiles covered their entire faces and ran over on the rest of us who had learned their story.

They gathered their small bags from overhead racks and headed hurriedly for the door and the freedom that is America.

I always stand tall when the National Anthem is played, but now I shall stand on tip-toes when the first notes of "O Say Can You See" fill whatever vacumn I'm standing in.

Memories

"The beautiful thing about memories," someone said, "is that you can enjoy experiences again and again and again."

"I was just sitting here thrilling," the aging lady announced as I entered her room filled with antiques and mementos of the past.

"You're doing what?" I asked.

"Just sitting here thrilling," she repeated, then explained by showing me her tattered folder of an ocean cruise she had taken decades ago.

Memories are wonderful but fickle. The bad memories haunt, kicking up renewed hostility and re-traumatizing. And good memories hurt even while warming us with past joys.

Christmas and New Years kick up many memories for everyone, because these two days (that cover a continuous season) are markers that stand as tall towers above the skyline of all the days and experiences that preceded them.

But memories are fickle. Your mind goes back to when the children were little. Thanksgiving was hardly turkey-ed away before they were in the attic dragging out Christmas trappings.

Then came the big day (usually Saturday) for trimming the tree (which had to touch the ceiling or it was not a bonafide Christmas tree!).

Furniture was rearranged or moved out for the season. The living room fireplace was filled with logs, which filled the room with warmth and brilliance.

With Christmas music playing on the stereo, you drag the tree trunk-first into the front hall with little chubby hands helping, but really only adding to your burden.

Then you string the lights, get a cup of coffee, and sit by while the family begins the ritual of placing favorite ornaments in special places.

Memories! Fickle. Past joys stir deeply in an empty spot down inside, churning warmness but also sadness over what was and can never be again.

Memories are fickle, and they are fatal if allowed to imprison rather than inspire. But if you can "sit there thrilling" while you drag the tree in unassisted, and the two of you trim it as you did your first one, then memories warm you and thoughts of their short Christmas visits will give present joy to anticipated togetherness.

May your memories be merry and bright.

December Praying

Lord, I simply need to talk with you.
It's December again and people are getting tired.
I see it in their eyes, hear it in their voices,
and feel it in their sharpness born of frustration.

It seems the whole world crashes in on us
  this time each year.
Schedules get filled but there's an emptiness about it all.
People work overtime, clerks get harried, shoppers get
  flustered and the whole mix of life takes on a brightness
   that does not glow.

Whaty is it all about, Lord?
People are supposed to be happy during the Christmas Season,
  or so everybody says.
And we feel guilty about not feeling all the joyful emotions
  we're supposed to feel.

Lord, what do I tell people? I'm your messenger, their
pastor.
What do I tell that wife whose husband died since last
  December?
And that husband who is in the same fix, knowing not the
  first thing about Christmas decorating or shopping
and couldn't care less?

And the little children, Father.
Those whose parents have divorced and they are wondering
  where and with whom they will spend this first Christmas
  after divorce court?

Do we have a word — any kind of word — for people living
  alone this Christmas?
Chairs about their tables are empty.
They can't bring themselves to bring out boxed-up
  decorations.

Something's locking them up.

I see fear in the eyes of people whose jobs have stopped
    and income shut off.
Father, there may be things worse than lost jobs,
    but jobless people have a hard time recalling what it is.
They are hurting.

So you see, Father, it is tough on many people right now.
And all those merry emotions they are supposed to feel
    only add to their burdens.

So what shall we tell them, Lord? Just hang tough? Hang on?
Shall we give them platitudes? "This too shall pass away?"
    "Cheer up and things will get better?"
Is that all we can say? Is there more?

What's that, Lord? Louder. You are in charge?
    Results are your business? Is that what you said?
Anything else? You love us? Suffer with us?
O.K., Lord. I hear that. Go where? Crib? Cross? Empty Tomb?

Thanks, Jeff

Jeff is my new friend. He's about five, that exciting, nothing-is-yet-impossible and full of faith age. Jeff and I were having a serious conversation shortly before Christmas.

"What are you going to get for Christmas?" I asked.

His eyes danced and a smile took over his entire face. "Everything!" he shouted, and stretched both arms to encompass the whole universe.

Adults standing in earshot smiled and perhaps parents would have urged him to be less general in his expectations, but I like exactly what Jeff said.

Thanks, Jeff, for reminding me that at Christmas we get everything. As you get older your theology may be more refined but it will not be any more defined than your five-year-old expression of what Christmas is all about.

Jeff, we did get EVERYTHING for Christmas. A lot more than the world can ever receive. We are given in that little Bethlehem Barn Baby everything that God can give us.

He has given us all sorts of promises — promises of peace

and love and joy and all the beautiful expressions and experiences we dream about.

As you get older, Jeff, you will come to know just how meaningful your definition of Christmas really is. It's an old, old story that is told and retold, but it becomes new everytime a little person like you begins to grasp what the Christmas gift is all about.

As you grow, Jeff, you will find that the "mass of things" at Christmas have less meaning than the "Christ of all things." He makes "things" in life have new meaning because we come to experience him in whatever things we hold.

Jeff, you may not understand all I'm saying, but that's what happens when we give someone a gift — we never know exactly what meaning it will have for them.

You gave me a gift by reminding me that I get "everything" for Christmas. And maybe some who read my "thank-you-note" will find that they too received EVERYTHING for Christmas.

So, Jeff, you see just how far a genuine Christmas gift can travel. Keep receiving EVERYTHING and keep giving what you receive. Thanks.

The Three R's

Rituals, rites, and routines. The Three R's of family life.

I didn't know they could be so important and strong. We have many rituals in our family, especially around Christmastime. And our two daughters — both young women now in their twenties — are determined that not one ritual or rite or routine shall ever be changed!

Every year the First Lady of our home approaches the subject of getting an "artificial tree this year." She has good reasons to support her position, but the two other ladies in our family offer their own reasons; and when their reasons are shot-down they simply close the subject with: "It would not seem like Christmas." End of discussion.

The multi-colored lights "have about had it," I tell everyone. Then I suggest the pretty little white lights — so much easier to put on the tree (my duty-contribution to decorating). "But Dad," protests the younger female, "I like to see all those colors gleaming through the window when I drive up to the house." And I journey to the marketplace for more colored bulbs.

Our tree must be real, big and round, touch the ceiling (whatever height the ceiling) and loaded with ornaments-gift-trinkets, hand-made, carried-over, worn-down, battered-around but bathed with memories too precious for neglect, too sentimental for words.

No gift can be opened prior to December 25, preferably at about 5:00 a.m. And no person can open a gift until a fire is crackling in the fireplace and the whole family is gathered around the tree.

On the first Christmas following our older daughter's marriage the younger informed her new brother-in-law that "The children all sleep together on Christmas Eve and sing songs until after mid-night."

Son-in-law's eyes widened, wondering how such a ritual would affect him. Discreetly they worked it out, and along about mid-night the familiar singing filled the house as another was baptized into the Three R's of the Smith household.

Rituals, rites, and routines. They are the glue that holds families together, giving a security of belonging, producing unity in family's feelings.

To Herod

"And Herod . . . was troubled." (Mt. 2:3) Big king troubled by birth of barn-baby in Bethlehem. What a newspaper headline!

Christmas still troubles people. Prices sky-high. Presents unbought and bought ones not yet wrapped. Aunt Susie's coming for the holidays and Lord only knows how long she'll stay!

But Herod's trouble stemmed from deeper concerns. He was an aging and angry ruler, third in the Herod Dynasty. For forty-plus years he had been King of the Jews; always powerful and sometimes good, he had been dubbed Herod-the-Great.

Nearing the end of his life he wanted to make sure no other prince or person would overthrow his dynasty. And when told by certain Wise Men that the "King of the Jews" had been born, this half-breed Jewish ruler felt threatening cold chills run through his sick, dying, and disturbed body and soul.

Herod started mountainizing molehills, an exercise in futility that will trouble any practitioner. Religious leaders, summoned for advice, misquoted or paraphrased Micah 5:2 and informed him the baby would "rule or govern" the people.

But the word is not "rule" but "shepherd." (Pastor) Herod, O Herod, that feed-box-baby only wants to pastor you! He wants to put arms of divine love around your human crookedness and make you straight; you and all your people and everybody's people.

Herod, he does not want to replace you; he wants to redeem you. He does not want to dethrone you, but to enthrone himself in your life so that you will be not merely Herod-the-Great but Herod-the-Greatest. Herod, that baby makes all people kings and they live in kingly splendor when they allow his kingship to shepherd their lives.

Don't be troubled, Herod. Be trusting. His kingship does not destroy; it discovers.

A Later Christmas

"Christmas is over." That declaration bothers me almost as much as the slogan plastered over retail store windows: "After Christmas Sale — Everything Half-Price."

Christmas is beginnings. It is a baby, and a baby is a beginning, a potential, something you watch. And in the context of Christmas that began in a barn and birthed the Christian gospel, there are no "after Christmas sales," let alone at half-price.

The little things that happen at Christmas birth in me simple but meaningful Christmas celebration. Oh, I love all the beautiful things that Christmas brings in terms of celebration: the church services, friendships renewed, families traveling for decorated homes where love is rekindled.

But sometimes it is the small, out of the way, barn-like incidents that touch deeply and are remembered longer than much-appreciated wrapped gifts.

Such an incident happened during our Children's Christmas Program on a Sunday afternoon. Our little ones had gathered and performed beautifully for our people, especially parents and grandparents.

As customary, I presented each child with a candy cane when they finished the program. One little fellow came back and asked for one.

"I thought I just gave you one," I said, smiling indulgently and ready to give him another because I had a surplus.

"You did," he confessed.

"Ah, you can have another," and I gave him one which he promptly hid by slipping it up his sleeve.

I thought no more about the incident until a few minutes later when he came back, pulled me aside, and said, "I wanted the candy for my sister. You see, she could not be in the program but she is here. I just wanted her to have one too."

The sincerity in the little fellow's eyes touched me deeply, and I wanted to give him the whole box!

It was not his or his sister's need for a single stick of candy (the family could afford truck loads if they so desired), but his genuine concern for his sister and his willingness to take whatever steps necessary so she would not feel left out that got to me and birthed the feeling that "this is what Christmas is all about."

Christmas is receiving, but receiving to share. And I hope that meaning is never "over" or "after" or "half-priced."

From The Innkeeper

No one knows my name. Only what I did, or didn't do, to be more specific. History records me only as "The Innkeeper" on that night of nights when angels and shepherds and smelly animals became famous. I became infamous. I did not give a room so that little baby could be born.

But you and history do not understand. You can't make a room or find a bed where there is none. Conditions were crowded. Oh, had I KNOWN I would gladly have given Mary and Joseph my room. But I didn't know. So I have gone down in history as the guy who refused God's son a place to be born.

On this anniversary of that night I want to say a word to you. Things are different now. You DO KNOW who it is that comes to be born in your life. You do not have the same excuse of ignorance that I claim. You have heard about him all your life, but many of you still use my old phrase, "There's no room."

I remember that night vividly. They did not push the issue. This God of ours never does. He simply knocks on the doors of our souls and offers us some need he has, but he doesn't force anything on us. He just stands there wanting to break into our lives with new life struggling to be born.

But God's truth will be born even if we refuse to be a part of it. He will go off into some remote arena where he can birth whatever truth he's laboring with. This God is never stymied by our refusal to participate with him. Oh, he could work much better with our positive response, but hardship has never stopped him.

He has a way of simply taking the negatives we often serve him and turning them around to suit his own will. And his will does prevail. That night his son was born nothing seemed right — hay dust, farm odors, all sorts of ungodly circumstances — but that night he made things right. In that little bundled barn baby a new moon was rising. New light for a darkened world was turned on. Redeeming grace dawned and this world has never been the same.

I knew nothing about any of this when I firmly and honestly announced, "There's no room in the inn." But in your day you know! Learn from my mistake. Make room for him. Let him be born IN YOU.

The room he wants is not in an inn; it's in you.

Baby or Person?

Melissa was eight years old and excited that her mother would soon give birth to a baby. Her excitement was bubbling over as she talked with her aunt about the coming event.

"Hey, that's neat," her aunt said. "You'll soon have a new person in your home."

"I don't want a person," she said, her face turning to a frown. "I just want a baby!"

The eight-year-old fairly well sums up what many people want in Christ and Christianity. They want a baby not a person. The temptation (at Christmas) is to reduce the Christian faith to a Bethlehem baby without realizing the baby grew to manhood, making certain demands based on the principle of mature love.

Don't read me wrong. The celebration of Christ's birth stands tall in my own experience and observance of Advent. I like the many actions of celebration that mark this season, complete with parties, family reunions, and especially the privilege of special worship opportunities.

But I also know the danger of failing to move from Advent of the God-Baby to events of the God-person.

As long as we can keep Jesus a baby we can avoid his teachings as a person. A baby can be handled, controlled, put to sleep, and generally manipulated for our own purposes and ends.

But it's rather difficult to exercise that same control and manipulation over a person. He talks back to us through his teachings, calling out the best in us and challenging the highest we have. And that stretches our minds, hurting-like.

Melissa, you're right. There's a difference between a baby and a person. And some parents try to keep babies from becoming persons, nursing them instead of nurturing them, coddling them rather than coping with their growing natures, and indulging their wants instead of inspiring them to discover their needs.

But such attempts backfire, producing pygmy parents and pygmy children.

And in the Christian faith the same thing happens. No crib or cross or tomb has ever confined the God-Baby who became the God-Person. He escapes every corner of confinement where our immaturity struggles to contain him.

Christmas is celebration of THE ADVENT. But growing Christian faith celebrates THE EVENTS that happen daily to those who faithfully look for new stars shining over old barns of personal experiences.

P.S.
Lines

Life's "et ceteras"

P.S. Lines
(Life's "et ceteras")
Rules and Friends

He shocked my thinking, or more accurately, shocked me into thinking.

"How many friends do you have?" he asked, making the question mark a sharp fish-hook instead of a simple mark of punctuation.

"Oh, I don't know," I said, attempting modesty rather than confession of ignorance.

"Give me a number," he urged, draining his coffee cup and signaling the waitress for more, acting smug, like he knew the exact answer and I didn't, or whatever I answered would be wrong. "Ten, five, three?" he asked, using fingers for visual aids.

"Oh, you know better than that. I've got a lot of friends," I defended, becoming a bit agitated at his low estimate of me.

"Seriously," he said, "How many real friends do you have? I mean, people who relate to you because of you, not because of your role or position or station in life?"

The question hung there, begging for attention and thought. We both creamed and sugared our fresh coffee in silence. Finally, he said, "Most of us can count on our fingers, one hand only, the number of real friends who would be our friends regardless of our position in life."

There's enough truth in my friend's evaluation to give pause for thought. He's probably right. Almost all of the people who relate to us on a daily basis do so because of the position or role we hold for them in life.

"She's not only my wife, but my friend," makes sense. The roles of husband and wife demand much role-playing, and rightly so. But the roles get rather thin, stilted, and boring unless husband and wife are genuine friends.

"My wife would be a close friend," declared a happy husband in sincerity, "even if we were not married." That says something about life, marriage, and friendship. Says a lot!

"He is not only my son, but my pal," makes sense, and gives insight into what family and friendship is all about.

Recently I stood with a twenty-five-year-old daughter whose mother was killed in an accident. "She was my best and closest friend," the daughter said as we turned to leave the funeral home.

When asked to name friends, many people never list their marriage mates and family. Yet this is where true friendship should and must exist, and maybe where it starts.

My friend is probably right. We have few genuine friends, but hundreds of friendly acquaintances who relate to us because of our roles and positions.

Friendship takes time and energy, and limitations of both prohibit cultivation of more than a few close, genuine friends. But, oh, aren't they worth all our investments?

Nominate and Campaign

The waitress finished pouring fresh coffee and my friend and I creamed and sugared it, stirring slowly.

"Some time ago," he said, "I heard you say that we nominate people to be our friends but they must elect whether or not they become our friends. Right?"

I nodded. "Something like that," I mumbled.

"Well, I have a friend who is really a friend. And that's exactly what he did. He nominated me for his friend but didn't stop there. Know what else he did?"

I didn't know and shook my head that way.

"He campaigned for election," and a big smile creased his face. "I'm glad he did and I'm glad he won the election."

"How did he campaign?" I asked, intrigued by the logical extension of the analogy.

"Oh, many ways. Invited me for golf, took me to his civic club, he and his wife invited us out to dinner and over to their home. Even took us on an overnight trip for a week-end of relaxation."

"That's good campaigning," I observed. "You liked that,

huh?"

"You'd better believe it. But he wasn't pushy. When we were invited but couldn't accept, they didn't seem hurt. They just gave us rainchecks and we went later."

My friend had experienced the basic law of making friends: We nominate a person for our friend but he/she must elect (freely) to become a friend.

Campaigning for election is a necessary and enjoyable part of the process. Merely to nominate, and never open doors (at least windows) through which relationship can happen, is to doom possible friendship from the beginning.

Nothing just happens. And friendship never just happens. Nomination, campaigning, and election cause friendship to happen.

When we moved to our new city, a person nominated me for his friend. He campaigned for election as my friend, doing many positive and helpful things for me.

And he won. I'm so glad he won. We filled two years full of friendship. Then suddenly a fatal heart-attack snapped his life, a man in the prime of life and only two years my senior.

I cried hard. It hurts deeply; one of the hardest funerals I've ever conducted.

He nominated, campaigned, and I elected. Thanks, Harold, for two years of friendship. You were an artist at friendship.

Touch . . . and BE

"Beauty is in the eye of the beholder," goes the famous quote. And we might add, "Beauty is also in the sensitivity of touch."

When a person comes alive to beauty, the sense of touch is quickened, giving added dimension to the ability TO BE.

There's the touch, feeling, of a good book's crisp new pages as you turn page after page, soaking up thought upon thought of the author's soul and mind.

And the touch of a dog's cold nose pushing against your hand, trying to get his strokes for the day. Or the Persian kitty, snuggling against your neck, just learning to use his purr-motor to melt whatever resistance you have to his impositions.

Then there's the feeling-touch of a three-year-old's tender

feet as you try to put socks on the squirming half-pint body cuddled in your lap.

What about the feeling of a two-year-old standing beside you in the car, arm around your neck, wiggling a stubby index finger in your ear as you try to negotiate the car through downtown traffic?

Oh, the touch — feeling — of a little hand (or larger one) of a loved one, rubbing the back of your neck, letting fingers gently dig into your hair, twirling it between four fingers and thumb.

What can be more tender, comfort more positively, than a hand laid on your hand when grief is cutting through your soul like the jagged edges of broken dreams?

And there's the feeling when you touch:

The smooth surface of solid walnut lumber you've just sanded for the custom-made piece of furniture in the workshop . . .

A well-worn football, just pumped up for the new season, when you grip it to throw to kids, now big as you, who you've been throwing to since they could barely walk. . .

And the touch of a wool scarf on a cold morning. . .

A hot coffee cup gripped with both hands. . .

Freshly washed and dried towel against your face . . .

The dignity of a heavily starched white shirt (and its coldness as you try to mold it to your neck and wrists). . .

The embrace of the person you've been married to for humpteen years, as exciting (and now more comforting) as it is familiar.

Thank God for what we experience through and with touch, and the ability to feel and BE!

Sounds Are Beautiful

When one of our daughters was little she called eyes "peepers." Some mornings when I tried to sleep late she'd come in and tenderly (at times roughly) try to open my eyelids. "Open your peepers," she'd command. Then gently she'd raise an eyelid, get close to me, and ask, "Anybody at home in there?"

That's a good question: "Anybody at home in there?" In short, anything going on in you? How alive are you? How aware to the sounds going on around you?

Sounds are beautiful, and their beauty involves more than hearing. The ability to see with an inward eye, to feel with an inward touch, is vitally involved.

Eyes are more than peepers, they are feelers; that is, if "somebody is home in there."

There's the sound of an outside door opening when you've been inside alone all day.

And the sound of, "Hi, Dad, how's my Pop?" humming along on long-distance telephone wires.

Then the sound of small feet pattering through the house like a herd of cattle in sudden stampede, and the genuine giggle when you take a little body in both hands, lift, hold close, and snuggle golden hair against your face.

Remember the muffled sound of kids trying to talk through ski masks, telling you it's their turn to ride on the snow sled; then, the crunch of fresh fallen snow under their booted feet as they move slowly like aged people because mother bundled them up so well?

Laughing. The sound of children laughing as they tell their secrets to each other, and you realize no matter how close you are to them, there's always a part of them you will never know because they are little human beings with a part of them marked off and labeled, "No Trespassing," and not even God violates that sanctity. And you smile, glad for the beautiful sound of laughing-secrets, signaling that your kids are normal, and on course in their development.

And there's the warm sound of metallic music coming from a chiming doorbell when you've been expecting the arrival of a close friend.

The sound of mail dropping into the box, giving notice that somebody's reaching out to you.

Suddenly, as you sit in the symphonic concert of daily sounds, it dawns on you that all these beautiful sounds involve people.

On Building Fires

Call it another Smith's Law, but I've found it true: "He who builds a fire warms himself twice, and often burns himself!" (Well, at least the last part is mine.)

It's happened to me many times. I love wood fires in dens. What is more restful and tranquil than a cold winter's evening, a crackling log fire, coffee brewing gently nearby, and the family lazily doing whatever.

By the time you get a fire laid — dry soft wood, paper, criss crossed splintered slabs, topped with large logs — you're warmed (if not hot and exhausted).

You strike a match and watch the first brilliant blaze of paper. Then wood catches onto the plan and does its thing. Soon the big logs get in rhythm with the evening's plans and, like proud men busting their buttons, throw out heat that moves you to a more distant spot in the room.

But sometimes things don't go exactly as planned. The paper burns out but the wood refuses. So you go poking around, repositioning first one log and then another. And nine times out of ten you burn yourself!

"He who builds a fire warms himself twice, and sometimes burns himself!"

And that's true in building fires in people, especially if you are a leader. And who isn't a leader is some area?

A person (or group) comes for help, or perhaps you are their leader. They need guidance, leadership, direction; in short, they need a fire built for them and in them.

You do your best. You teach, lead, stimulate, and hope somehow to strike a flame of personal motivation within them. Sometimes it works; it happens. The fire catches and burns. And you are twice-warned: first, by stimulating and teaching others you learn perhaps more than you teach. Second, you see them motivating and moving on their own, and that warms you.

But often it backfires or doesn't fire just right; and you get burned in the process. Sometimes the person to whom you give your best energies and most attention burns you after the process if not during it. (That involves the negative dynamics of dependency which I'm not prepared or purposed to discuss here.)

Parents often get burned as they build fires of stimulation, motivation, and expectation in their children. (It happens also between husband and wife in marriage.)

Every leader is in the fire-building business. He should anticipate being twice warmed and expect to be many times burned. (Comes with the territory . . . er, fireplace.)

Last Minute People

"I'm a last minute person," he declared with some degree of pride. "I always get the job done, but I might wait to the last minute."

I resent such a philosophy, and get on the verge of anger toward such practitioners.

Look at that statement for a moment. The person is saying several things about himself.

First, he reveals he's in some kind of childhood rebellion not yet resolved even though he may be fifty-years-old. People who constantly "are late" are resisting something or rebelling against something. Of course, every person is entitled to his own pet rebellion.

But when such patterns infringe upon the time and energy of another person's rights and schedules, then a whole new ballgame is ushered in.

The last minute person is selfish, refusing to see that other people may be dependent on him doing his job before they can do theirs.

I have seen entire organizations stopped because one person (a last minute person) had not got his work in on time.

Last minute people who are executives are the worse culprits. They rush into the office, dictate a letter that must be out by five, while the clock shows 4:55 and secretaries are already pulling covers on typewriters.

It happens in the home all the time. "Please mow the lawn, son. I want to fertilize but I can't until the lawn is mowed."

Last minute son says, "Dad, I always get it done. Just give me time."

So he's given time. Long about dark he finishes. But you don't spread fertilizer on dew drenched grass. So Dad's project halts. (Plus, the next day it rains and Dad's whole fall fertilizing project is off schedule.)

"I want to clean the kitchen and start the dishwasher and get out of here," pleads one sister to another.

"Give me time. I'll do my job. But when I'm ready," announces last minute sister.

And on the list goes of people trapped in the last minute syndrome, while standing by are all those whose jobs, plans, hopes and dreams wait. Halted. Stymied.

A last minute person is in rebellion against something. He ignores the worth of others, sets himself up as the universe's center, and is oblivious to the rights, privileges and plans of other people.

P.S. At times we all are last minute persons. But this should be a rarity, not a pattern. If it's a pattern, let me suggest several good counselors!

How Many Bites?

He was a young man, about twenty five. I watched as he gathered his tools after installing carpet in our home.

"A good job," I said. He thanked me. "You've laid a lot of carpet," I observed, judging by the good job he had done.

"Yes, sir, sure have."

"How long does a piece of carpet like this last?" I asked, as much to make conversation as for information.

"Well, sir," he said, smiling. "I don't mean to sound sassy, but let me put it this way: How many bites in a sandwich?"

"'Nuff said," I laughed. "I get your point."

Long after the young carpet-layer had gone, his philosophical statement remained, haunting, pricking, kicking up all sorts of thoughts, analogies and applications.

Just HOW MANY bites are there in a sandwich? As many or as few as I decide, I guess. And life is put together pretty much like that.

Often I am asked similar questions:

How long to get through the grief of a death, or a divorce, or the loss of a job?

How long to spend time on one's child?

How long to keep trying to make it in a marriage floundering like the Titanic?

How long to get through the empty-nest syndrome?

How long to keep on forgiving family members or friends before you wear out or become calloused?

And my answer, if I'm really honest, should be: How many

bites in a sandwich? No one really knows. It's different for different people. You can make it as long or as short as you decide. There are some things in life for which there are no patterns or guidelines. So many things depend upon one's individuality.

We have dietary principles and suggestions for just about everything in life except one: "How many bites in a sandwich?" That's one thing that's negotiable; you can take as many or as few as you like.

Living in the context of family there are certain things that are negotiable, and can be determined by each person according to his best knowledge, wisdom and judgment.

How many bites in a sandwich? I have no earthly idea. But two things I do know: too few bites and I get indigestion: too many bites and I give other people (who are waiting for me to finish) indigestion!

Joe-Horse Philosophy

Joe was the horse my friend Cliff and I bought jointly for our children. He never won any beauty contests nor races, but he was a gentle old creature our kids loved and spent many afternoons astride.

We boarded Joe at a barn on the outskirts of the city, but Cliff and I had to provide feed and keep his stable clean.

The story my friend and fellow horse-owner tells goes like this. He'd call and say Joe needed feed. And according to Cliff I'd say, "Well, that's your half of the horse."

Then Joe's stable would need cleaning. Cliff would call informing me of that bit of bad news. My response, as Cliff remembers, was, "That's your half of Joe."

"Which half of Joe do you own?" he supposedly asked one day in exasperation.

He says I replied, "The half in the middle where the saddle fits."

I don't exactly remember coming right out and saying that, but if I'm honest, I sorta felt that way. And maybe I acted that way at times. Anyhow, Cliff was patient with me and we are still best of friends, in spite of Joe, horse feed, and stable manure.

I guess, if the truth is admitted, many of us live out our lives in home, community, and job with my Joe-Horse Philosophy. We take our stands in life right in the middle, wanting only to sit in the saddle, avoiding both ends that demand investment and work.

Yet life is made up of all three. Somebody must make investments to insure food. I recall that sometimes Cliff and I would drive over the countryside for hours trying to locate farmers who'd sell us hay for Joe.

And somebody has to clean the stable. There are many unpleasant tasks in this business called life. No one has the right to impose all stable work on another person.

It simply boils down to this: If you want to enjoy sitting in the saddle then you have to buy and lug hundreds of pounds of feed into the barn, and grab a pitchfork and shovel and clean the stable.

Then, and only then, can you justly throw on the saddle and ride over the countryside with the wind in your face and heavy cares behind you.

Rivers

What does the Dead Sea and a dry pond have in common? Both are useless! Good examples of bad situations. They represent the extremes of taking in too much and giving out too much. They lack balance, rhythm.

For centuries the Dead Sea has provided illustration for moral sermons, a salty example of selfishness. It takes in and never gives out. And it deserves the Dead designation.

But what about the dry pond? Not many homilies on this one. Yet a dry pond is as useless as a Dead Sea.

It goes to the opposite extreme, constantly giving out but not taking in.

The Dead Sea syndrome infects people with constant self-getting. Self-improvement becomes an obsession. Individualism with the theme song, "I'll Do My Thing — Only," becomes primary.

Danger of Dead Sea-ness surfaces whenever a person sacrifices family and community in favor of personal accomplishment. The deadliness of Dead Sea-ism is not at the point of gathering, but at the point of not sharing.

Meanwhile, back at the dry pond, likewise a syndrome of no less deadliness. Its sickness comes not from being locked up and closed, but from being locked in the open position! Everything goes out and nothing comes in.

Dry pond-ness is sharing, serving, and working in behalf of everyone and all good causes without ever taking time to study, renew, re-create and replenish one's energies and reserves.

Dry pond-ism wears its heels out on errands of mercy and good deeds, but neglects the soul and its culture. It trades the shoe-leather of service for the gray-matter of study.

Dead Sea or dry pond? Our only options?

No, there is another. It's the free flowing river that combines intake from springs of learning with give-outs of sharing.

And as the old spiritual sings it: "I've got peace, joy, love like a river."

Shelf-List

Steven told me he is four, and tightened his thumb hard against his palm and stuck up four fingers to support his claim. And he's talkative. Not "in-the-way" talkative, but communicates. Likes people. Had known me only a few minutes and had given and taken our respective histories.

"Where's your buddy?" I asked, inquiring about his little friend who had come with him.

"In the other room," he said, articulating with typical four-year-old impediments. "I'll go get him," he volunteered.

In a minute he was back. "He won't come," Steven reported in disgust.

"Why?"

"He's shelflist."

"He's what?" I asked.

"Shelf-list," he repeated, drawing out the word.

"Oh, selfish," I said, correcting his pronunciation.

"Yeah, shelflist," he agreed.

I smiled at the little fellow's mispronunciation, but he gave me a new definition of the word.

"Shelf-list." That's exactly what "selfish" is or does. It put Steven's little friend on a shelf and kept him from enjoying what Steven and I had going on in the room.

Selfishness always does that. It puts us on a shelf by ourselves, cutting us off from other people. It takes us out of the mainstream of what's happening in life and community.

Selfishness takes us out of circulation, causes us to withdraw into ourselves, and we are never touched by the warm fires burning in the souls of other persons. It often insulates us from the storms of life but also from the cool breezes that blow fresh, new life into us.

Now, I don't think Steven's little friend missed all that much by not coming along with us, but I know "shelf-listness" often puts our names on a "list" that is labeled OFF-LIMITS so far as other people are concerned. Stay on the shelf too long and soon people no longer reach out to us. They quit bothering about us.

And the worst thing in the world is to be ignored, left alone, by-passed. All of this usually happens when we put ourselves (for whatever reasons) on the shelf of life.

We are social beings, created for community, not isolation. The greatest crime we commit against the image of God in which we are created is withdrawal.

Shelf-listness.

Woosley

Donald Woosley Waggoner (he likes "Woosley," but most people call him "Don") is perhaps more intellectual than the rest of us on the staff put-together. He's certainly the most interesting, intriguing, and fascinating; plus, you never know what he will come up with next.

Don is our parking lot attendant (Automobile Arrangement Specialist, he says). Under contract to the church's commercial custodial service, he also mows the lawn and keeps the whole area manicured.

"Woosley" is an avid reader, and can discuss in depth almost any theologian, philosopher, certainly every playwright. Having crossed the half-century mark, he has played on Broadway, understudied some big names, and in the last two decades has starred in major drama productions that merited him high praise from media reviews.

And, above all, he is a drama director, holding many successful credits. Recently he founded ACTORS COMPANY THEATRE (ACT) that produces plays in the basement of our church. (*Androcles and the Lion, Christmas Carol, Foxfire, The Miracle Worker,* and *Charlotte's Web.*) And on the agenda for the next year is: *Sherlock Holmes, The Night Thoreau Spent in Jail, Scrooge and Marley, MacBeth,* and *Life With Father.*

"Woosley," I asked some years ago. "Why this job? Why not go on to something bigger?"

"Sir," he said, serious and minus the usual humor that constantly saturates his conversations. "I'm happy. I like what I'm doing. It gives me time to do ALL I like to do. After all," he said, fixing his sharp eyes squarely on mine, "isn't this what life's all about? Fulfillment?" I never raised the question again.

Don's notes to me are classics. I file every one of them. Recently, during the windy days of March, I told my secretary to inform Don that trash had blown all over the church's yard.

Here's his reply (personally typed):

> Dr. Smith:
>
> Well, sir, I come in last Saterde and got the church yard lookin' rite good.
>
> Then the blow come on Monday. Becky (pastor's secretary) says you wanted her to remind me to pick up the junk.
>
> Well, sir, it was like this. I chased a Pepsi Cola can up to 16th St. (four blocks) before I caught it. I lost two Miller Lite cans in Guyandottee (two miles east) so I just give up.
>
> But I'll sure keep after it.
>
> (Signed) Love, Woosley Waggoner
Star Directore
Producer and all round
good guy.

Thanks, Donald WOOSLEY Waggoner. You prop us up on our leaning side.

Humility

His name is T.H. Broyhill, older of the two brothers who founded Broyhill Industries, a major manufacturer of furniture in the world.

My dad worked for him during the struggling years of the company's infancy. Mr. Tom, as he was affectionately called, was a fine man, sensitive to the needs of people and community. I admired him, but often stood in awe of his wealth and reputation. (That was my problem, not caused by him.)

At the end of my freshman year in college, I was saying goodbyes to my friends around the campus. I spotted Mr. Tom (a trustee of the college, there for a trustee meeting and graduation exercises) talking with a man whose clothes and general appearance indicated modest background and means.

I stood for a time in earshot of the two conversing men, waiting for a chance to speak to Mr. Tom.

I heard the stranger ask Mr. Tom, "What do you do for a living?"

Mr. Tom sputtered a bit, shifted his weight, and said, "My family makes a little furniture."

"I fool with furniture some," the stranger replied. "Made two splitcane rocking chairs last month. Sell 'em to tourists coming through here."

The conversation continued with both men talking about making furniture. But not one time did Mr. Tom ever indicate who he was or what kind of furniture enterprise he had going. The stranger never knew he stood in the presence of one of the world's foremost manufacturers of furniture.

When someone asks for a definition of humility, I tell that story. Mr. Tom did not make the other fellow feel badly or inferior by reciting how great a furniture empire he was a part of. Nor did he put the less-fortunate person at a personal or professional disadvantage. He didn't make him feel stupid or less important.

And Mr. Tom asked the man in detail about making splitcane rockers. "Just how," I heard him ask the stranger, "do you go about making that wood bend to suit you?"

The man told him. And Mr. Tom listened intently. Humility is being open to what another person can teach you, and respecting the potential in every person.

Interruptions

Sometimes I hear stories that are just that — stories; true, good, and lend themselves to no particular application of the moment. I've got some I need to tell.

There's one about R.L. Patton, a leading educator of another day, who grew up in my home area. He became a respected teacher and enjoyed a brilliant career in the early days of awakening education in my native state.

His mother died when he was in his late teens. He and his new step-mother had problems getting along with each other. She was demanding and perhaps insensitive to his needs. And he no doubt rebelled at some of her demands.

One day she ordered him to bring in some firewood. He flatly refused, whereupon his father stepped into the situation and ordered him, in no uncertain terms, to get the wood.

The young Patton went toward the woodpile but kept going. He ended up at Amherst College in Massachusetts where for the next four years he studied and earned his degree.

Following graduation he returned home, and on the way into the house, picked up the load of wood he had been ordered to get four years before!

There's another related story about my late friend, Carlyle Marney. During his pastorate at Myers Park Baptist Church in Charlotte he suffered a heart attack in the middle of his sermon.

It was many weeks later that he had recovered enough to enter the pulpit again.

His opening statement was: "As I was saying . . ."

I love the sense of humor and perspective that both leaders possessed. There's a sense of "real-ness" in both experiences and expressions of life.

Another interruption happened during a Baptist Convention in a civic center. The large hall had an orchestra pit that could be raised and lowered for effective presentations.

The program committee had a great time with the unusual facility and would bring up the various presentations via the elevator-type floor.

During an address by a visiting dignitary someone accidently hit the wrong switch and the entire floor, guest speaker and all, started going down into the basement.

Just as the speaker was about to disappear, he smiled and waved goodbye.

Humor. Humor of perspective. I love it.

Waves

It was one of those early mornings, just after sunrise, days at the beach when the wind was barely moving the limber sea oats. You could sight a wave in the making as far to your left as you could see, then follow it down the beach as it piecemeal-ed itself on the shore.

The cup of coffee warmed chilled hands and the scene stimulated the waking mind. The waves became long lines of heritage as they spent themselves on the sandy coast. Like grandparents of the past, the wave caught your eye, far to the left, losing itself and becoming one with the sand.

Following the wave down the coastline you could see immediate history being made as it white-capped itself just before breaking into the past.

As your eyes moved with the water's momentum it was but a swell, promising to break and give itself to spraying power in its moment of glory.

Like looking into the future, you could see the beginning hump of a mounting wave gaining power to break and spend its one, glistening moment on the stage of history. And now your eye could no longer behold what you knew had to be out there, and coming.

Wave after wave came, reminding you that life is a parade of movement. You can see but a glimpse of its beginning and a foretaste of its end. And somewhere in the long line stands you, gifted of the past, graced in the present, and granted a future by faith.

There's perspective on life's moving moments as you drain the last drops of coffee that have become chilled; but now the sun warms you in a way coffee never can.

But maybe the warmness is neither from sun nor coffee but the realization that you are part of a long, mounting and break-ing wave that has given you a uniqueness in the vast ocean of history.

There is a continuity of life and history, of family and community, that makes relationship to each a "thing of beauty and a joy forever."

And you hope, as you turn from the reflective moment spent at God's special altar, that somehow in your moment of breaking and cresting, you will give enough of yourself to make your moment in history a contribution of purpose. And your place in the continuing wave-line a promise of legacy.

An Hour Gift

I've been given an extra hour that has multiplied. It all started when we went from daylight savings time to standard and I turned back the clocks on the wall, wrist, car, office, upstairs, downstairs, stove . . . Fact is, I almost used up the hour getting the clocks reset.

But not quite. Not by a long shot! The only clock I cannot get turned back is the one inside me.

My 6:00 a.m. getting-up-time is now 5:00. But my going-to-bed clock still likes 11:00 p.m., or later. And I'm caught in the squeeze.

So the day is longer but exciting. It's amazing what can happen with that one extra hour. Ah, the freshness of the morning while it is still black outside (as it is now as I write). No jarring telephone to break the spell; no cars droning; just quietness broken only by silent thoughts moving quickly into the consciousness for assimilation.

One extra hour per day means almost one extra working day per week. And thirty extra hours per month; that's 365 extra hours per year or more than two extra weeks of 24-hour days or 45 8-hour working days. The possibilities blow the mind.

That may be the answer to: "I wish there were more hours in the day." There are. It really boils down to ARRANGEMENT, or for most of us, re-arrangement.

Of course, the real question is: what shall I do with this extra hour? Merely more of the same? Or shall I do something different with this new gift?

I've decided that for one hour per day I will do something different. No, I'm not telling what because I hope to change it often if not every day. I refuse to allow this new gift to become routine or rutted like so many of my hours become.

But, alas, I have a fear. It is the fear or fact that after a few weeks I will absorb the hour into "the daily run of duty" and miss its grace.

God's new gifts often become victims of such fate. And routine results in boredom and boredom births loneliness and loneliness becomes the parent of depression and depression is deadly.

But maybe, just maybe, I will allow this new gift to make me acutely aware of ALL GOD'S GIFTS. Ah, there's the gift of beauty — trees, flowers, the changing seasons. And the beauty of family and friendship. What would a friendless world be like? (Hope I never learn.)

One extra hour with 60 beautifully wrapped minutes to open and pack full of God's greatest gift: Life!

Freedom and Love

Smokey is our cat. As I write this article he is snuggled smugly in the out-going mail tray on my desk. In a few moments, as is his custom, he will move to my typewriter, purr for attention, then simply walk on the keys to make sure I am aware of his presence.

But Smokey is not REALLY my cat. He belongs to Rachel, our youngest daughter, who has taught me not only to tolerate cats but to love them. Yet the family agrees he's actually my cat. He follows me around, cries for my attention, sits on my lap, and generally expresses undying love for me, much to the chagrin of his legitimate owner.

I guess it goes back to the day we got Smokey. Rachel and I went to the Animal Shelter looking for a cat. She found one she liked and had started toward the desk to buy him. But just then this gangly, bluish-gray adolescent reached through the cage-bars and caught my sleeve, pulling me to him.

I opened the iron-bound prison that confined him and took him in my arms, stroking him. He responded with genuine catty-enthusiasm.

I called Rachel's attention to Smokey (the name appearing on his cage). She wasn't impressed. So she put him back, but as she turned to leave, he reached out again through the bars, caught her sweater, and pulled her to him. The smile on her face told me Smokey was making progress. Once again I opened the door, took him out, and gave him to her. That did it. We paid the $5.25 (including tax) and Smokey became her cat.

But from day-one he has related more to me than other family members. And after nearly four years the family has concluded that he is really my cat because I set him free. Yet I doubt that merely "setting him free" from his cage is the complete answer. I did set him free BUT I ALSO gave him love and attention.

Freedom without love produces chaos; freedom with love generates relationship, even with a cat. How much more with human beings. (And nations.)

Bigger And . . .

I'm convinced that BIGGER is not always better, but it is always more INCONVENIENT! To wit, telephone service today. As I write, our telephone is dead; deader than a door-nail (however dead that is).

There was a day (not many months ago) when all I had to do was call the local people from a neighbor's phone, and pleasant voices assured immediate, if not sooner, attention and service.

Not so now! I called a suspicious, unfamiliar-sounding number with no one's area code attached and still reached a pleasant-sounding voice promising attention sometime tomorrow between the hours of eight and seven.

No, she told me, not today. The computer will set the service calls in motion, but it has already done its assignment for today, she reported. We are sorry for the inconvenience, she assured me, but was grateful I had called you-know-who. (She did say that if the inconvenience proved harmful to me or any member of the family they would make other arrangements. That was nice.)

Well (to coin a phrase), there's no way we can put Ma Bell's Humpty-Dumpty fall back together. We can't retrace our steps, even as many as would like to do so. All the king's horses, and all the king's men, cannot turn back the clock (or dial) to the yesteryears when merely a simple distress call brought immediate attention.

Everything's getting bigger and more INCONVENIENT. What is one to do? Write-out frustration in a book (like you-know-who)? Or simply fume and fuss at no one in particular. PATIENCE may be the answer. Fact is, it IS THE ANSWER. And it is not patience born of virtue; it is patience born of necessity.

But perhaps the only way I get patience (which is an inward experience and attitude) is to learn it and practice it even when I don't need it — especially when I don't need it. This makes patience a virtue; and it re-births itself in times of necessity.

In I Cor. 13 Paul says: "Love is patient and kind." That is, patience is an inward experience that issues into kind actions. So, I will not jerk my phone from its socket; nor be unkind to that pleasant voice and her computer hundreds of miles away.

I'll try not to!

Many Cold, Few. . .

Minus 16. Sixteen degrees below zero. -16 F. Anyway I write it, it still comes out COLD. Terribly cold; bone-chilling cold; stay-in-the-house cold.

Add the wind chill factor and my mind cannot even think in such figures. (Wish they hadn't come up with that bit of measurement. It didn't seem nearly so cold until I learned about that!)

How cold was it? That's how cold it was recently — 16 below being frozen.

Then it warmed up to 21 above zero. A real heat wave. Seriously, it seemed so much warmer that I started peeling off layered clothing. But the weather was still capable of freezing me — to death under certain circumstances.

It was the contrast between what I had experienced and what I was experiencing that made me feel warmer. My body had conditioned itself; my brain was accomodating my feelings, or was it the other way around?

Whatever, the temptation to do certain outside-things surfaced, promising relief from a growing cabin-fever. But the danger of freezing was still there, regardless of MY FEELINGS.

When you live long enough in sub-zero weather the body adjusts; then, when the temperature rises to a mere 21-degrees above zero, the body gives mixed, if not wrong, signals.

It is then that we must trust the thermometer, not our feelings. Feelings will get you frozen.

Feelings are important in life, but they cannot always be trusted because they are conditioned by the environment.

If I am exposed long enough to a negative moral environment, chances are my feelings will be so conditioned that I will not sense the destructive elements around me.

This is when I best look at the thermometer of my value-system and permit its moral signals to guide my actions, even though my feelings tell me something else.

Feelings are at best a barometer of great pressures, but not a guide in dealing with moral weather.

Nails and Torn Britches

I heard it on television, that invader of the home which someone has predicted will give us a generation of people with eyes the size of grapefruits and brains the size of English peas; baby English peas!

An elderly, philosophical farmer (is there any other kind?) was being interviewed by a news commentator. I don't remember the issue being discussed, but it had something to do with a mistake the farmer had made farming.

The newsman asked if he'd ever do that (whatever it was) again?

"No sir," he said, rubbing his overalls. "I don't tear my britches on the same nail twice!"

Right on! What a philosophy of life, and what a hard principle to live by! Yet, the essence of maturity is learning from our mistakes, and learning not to make the same mistake twice.

Someone has observed that "the only thing we learn from history is that we don't learn from history." Lot of truth there. But certainly one should learn from one's own history, even though we refuse (incapable?) to learn from the history of the generations before us.

Patterns are difficult to change, but I'm convinced they can be changed. Some say basic personality characteristics cannot be changed. Maybe not. But I contend they can be rechanneled, brought to positive maturity, and mellowed. If this is not true, then much of what we are doing in education, religion, psychology and industry is just so much effort and energy down the drain.

Two things can be learned from "torn britches." One, know where THAT nail is and stay away from it. Two, there are MANY nails in life just waiting for us to tear our britches on them.

Or, put another way: learn HOW we made the mistake, and WHAT did the mistake teach us. No experience is ever wasted unless we allow it to be. And that includes tearing britches on waiting nails.

Maturity could be defined as learning not to tear your britches on the same nail twice!

Checkbooks, Socks, and Marriage

"It saved our marriage," she said, then related an event that seemed insignificant to me but terribly important to her, her husband, and their marriage.

After nearly three decades of marriage I can't say that any-one-thing "saved" our marriage (it hasn't been on the verge of dying that many times!) but there are two LITTLE things that have made it smoother.

THe first one was a lost checkbook. During the first years of marriage we had a joint checking account and two little pocketsize checkbooks. The arrangement was convenient, easy, and enabled us to write checks at will and on the spot. And it provided us with telephone calls from the bank about the 20th of each month! We never knew the balance in our account. And that will take romance right out of any relationship.

Then one of us (I'll not tell who) lost a checkbook. (Divine Providence does have a way of "saving.") We started using only one book. Later, we graduated to a large, commercial checkbook that is too big for the desk, let alone carry around.

(Footnote: We still don't have much more money at the end of the month, but we do know how little we have. And that's helpful even if not comforting.)

The second discovery concerns my SOCKS. Now, there's one

important thing about socks: It takes two! One for each foot, and identical.

But our washing machine contains the original "Black Hole." It has a way of eating socks; not, mind you, a PAIR of socks, but rather ONLY ONE sock from each pair. Consequently, I am the proud owner of about 60 socks that have experienced divorce from their mates. (If you have two feet there's not much you can do with one sock.)

Another related problem has to do with the difficulty of determining dark-blue socks from dark-black socks when taking them from the washing machine, based, of course, on the assumption they survive said washing machine's appetite. (I'll not even mention the feeling of sitting on the platform and discovering a black sock on your left foot and you-know-what on your right.)

But we discovered a little, inexpensive plastic ring that requires only a second to insert a PAIR of socks into its snug grip, a grip that survives washing machine's thieving efforts. (Of course, I may be losing an entire pair now. But the frustration of the ONE-SOCK syndrome has been eliminated.) And, too, the washed socks are easily matched. They hang together.

Marriages are not made of large checkbooks for joint bank accounts or matched socks that survive washing cycles, but the mornings are smoother and there are fewer calls from the bank.

No Penny, Please

The man's life was definitely "fast-lane," yet his lifestyle seemed positive. He worked long hours, out-performed his peers, and generally exhibited an energy level few people could match. Sometimes he seemed like "a man driven."

"What's going on with him?" I asked his close friend.

"He's got a penny behind his fuse."

"He's got a what behind his what?" I asked.

My friend laughed, then reminded me than in old houses there were fuse boxes that contained "plugs" that were installed and would blow-out if the electrical overload was too much.

Sometimes, he said, people did not have plugs to replace the blown ones and would simply place a penny behind the plug.

Of course, the electricity would flow but the safety feature of the plug was eliminated. "Dangerous," he observed, "but it did provide lights for the house."

He applied the analogy to his friend. "He's simply got a penny behind his fuse. He operates with all safety features removed. His energy flows uninhibited. I'm not sure how long he will last before he burns himself out."

"Burn-out," common word today for exhausted people, is caused by putting pennies behind our mental, physical, and spiritual fuses. The power flows, and we stretch our working days far beyond the normal safety limits.

But what happens when the overload becomes too much? Do we, like the old electrical installations, burn up the house rather than blow a fuse? Perhaps.

My friend (the expert on fuse plugs) said that "putting pennies behind fuses" is okay in an emergency, but can be fatal if left there too long."

An occasional sixteen-hour day is often necessary in tight times. But to make it a lifestyle is to put a "penny behind the fuse."

Pardon me while I take a look at my own fuses!

Non-Essential Persons?

"Non-Essential Persons Given Afternoon Off!" All 500,000 of them, or so stated the news release when the Federal Government almost went out of business recently.

That's a terrible designation — "Non-essential persons." I don't know all the problems faced by federal authorities in their action, but to call any person non-essential grates, rubs something raw inside me.

With government's ability to come up with all sorts of special names for agencies (some of them weird), it appears to me a more humane and less de-humanizing designation could have been birthed.

Wonder how the husband and father of four children felt when he walked into his home that fateful afternoon? "Mom," calls a youngster. "Our non-essential daddy is home!"

What does a loving husband say over dinner to his bride who packed her essential belongings and trapsed from the office with "non-essential" emotionally stenciled on her forehead?

I'd have difficulty the next morning when non-essentials were called back to work. Perhaps I'd stare long and hard at whatever tasks I'd left unfinished. "Why do it, let alone hurry," would have to cross my mind as "non-essential" played around in my head with sharp and barbed edges.

Who is essential in an organization and who is non-essential? If the president of a company — and certainly he'd be considered essential — is absent from his desk for two weeks, most people in the organization may hardly note his absence.

But let the janitor be gone two days!

The physician can take several days off, but the aide who empties bedpans and changes bed linen? You do get the idea?

"I take my job seriously," the aging custodian of our church said to me years ago. He elaborated: "I don't care how great a preacher you are. If people have to sit in dusty pews they will never hear a word you say." That conversation began an immediate and lasting friendship, and mutual respect for the essential nature of our respective responsibilities.

Simon Peter (Acts 10:28) puts the whole thing into focus: "God has shown me that I should not call any man common."

And we might add: "Nor non-essential."

Summer Guests

With the coming of spring, we have several guests returning who "summer" at our place. During this past winter we did not see nor hear from them because they were wintering in central South America.

But now they are back. Their antics, lifestyles, habits and routines fascinate me as I watch quietly through our breakfast-room picture window.

And what a picture the window gives! God's magnificent creation, the little hummingbird, sometimes is nothing more than a blur as he races about thirty miles per hour (and he can go up to fifty or sixty when he is in a hurry), then hovers to extract sugared-water from the glass feeder.

He's no more than 3½ inches long and weighs (on a full stomach) about a tenth of an ounce. But what an eater he is!

The average man burns about 3500 calories a day, while the hummingbird burns 150,000 per day. To keep up with the hummingbird, a man would need to eat 400 pounds of meat and starch just to stay even. The hummingbird must eat every twenty minutes or he is in trouble.

The hummingbird's pulse beats 450 times per minute when he's at rest. But when he's moving around it goes to 1,250 times per minute.

He's the only bird that can hover, fly backwards, but cannot soar. He intimidates other birds, driving them from feeding areas.

When the hummingbird wants to go somewhere, his short, little feet are of no value. He cannot hop or walk, not even for short distances. He's totally dependent on his wings that beat some 70 times per second in a figure eight pattern.

While not an expert on hummingbirds, I have become intrigued by this almost-smallest of God's creative genuis. Nature is not the source nor end of my God-worship, but it does provide provoking thoughts upon our Creator's sense of detail, beauty, and the extraordinary.

And for only a few dollars for a feeder and a few cents for one-part sugar, four-parts water, and a dash of red food coloring, I can stand amazed in the presence of this little bird and its Creator-God.